Introduction

This book shares a visual journey over a period of few months during my visit to India in December 2018. I had photographed these images while traveling in the north and on the western coast of India.

Flipping through the book, each page depicts the experience of a beginner photographer and the excitement of exploring and documenting the land which has preserved its colours and culture over the past thousands of years.

Majority of the images are from Gujarat, as it was my first visit to the western coast, hence a lifelong memory and a collection. At the time I just got into photography and with Canon 1300 D as my first dslr, the photographs are a mix of a DSLR and iphone.

Some Locations:

New Delhi, Gujarat (Dwarka, Beyt Dwarka, Somnath, Porbandar), (Noorpur, Deoband), (Phillaur, Punjab).

Karn Kalia
31-07-2021

Delhi, the journey begins...

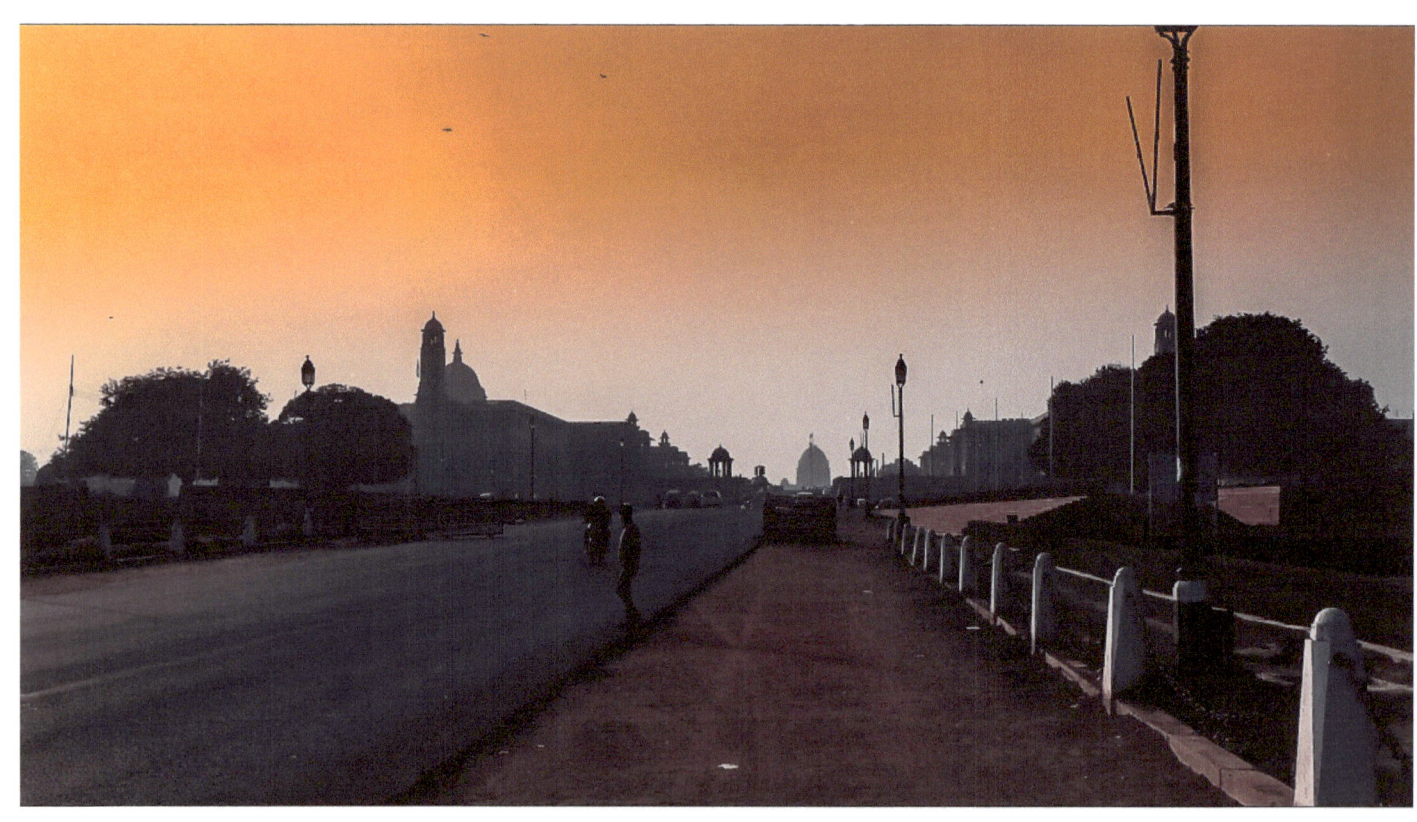

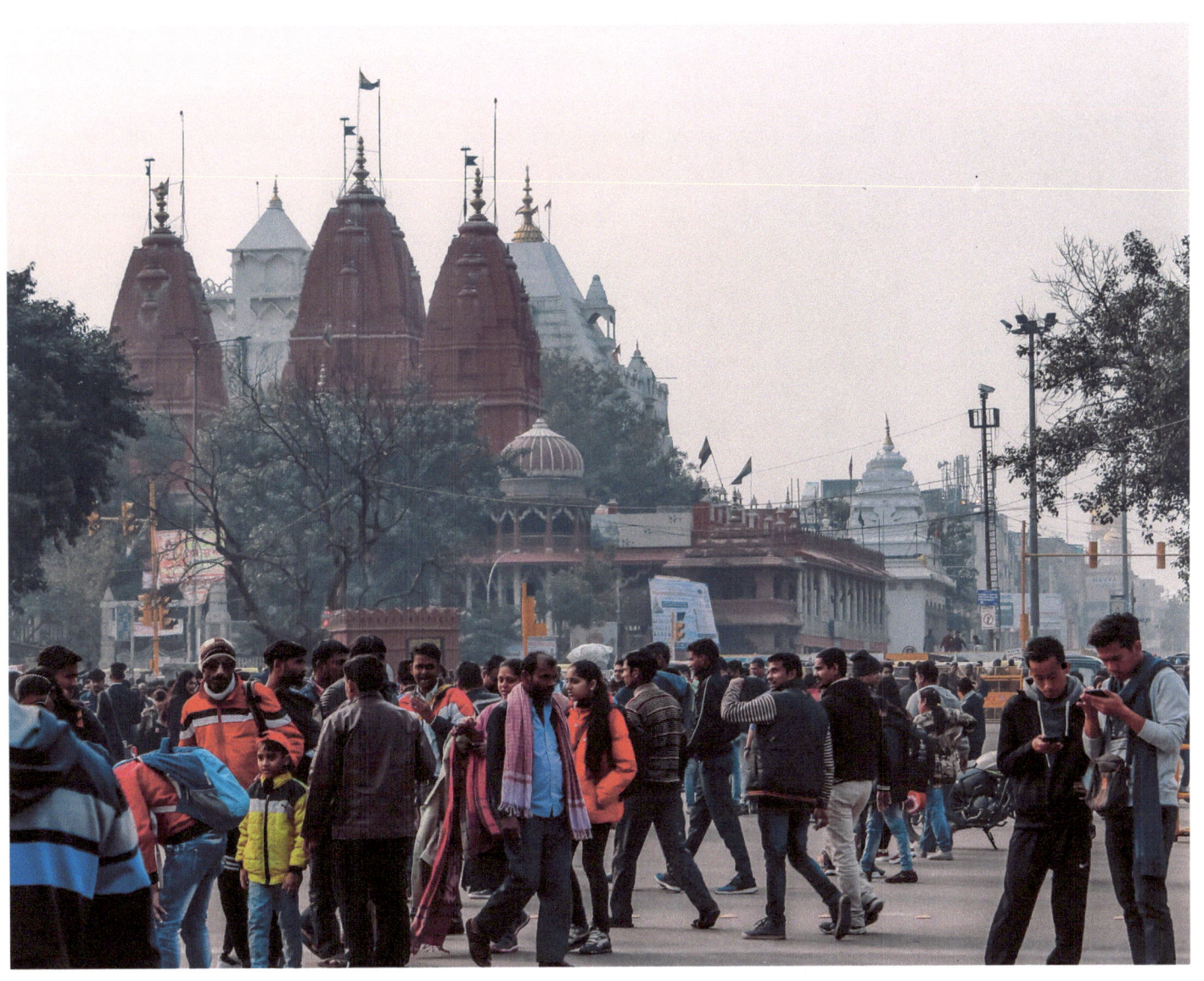

Agrasen ki baoli...

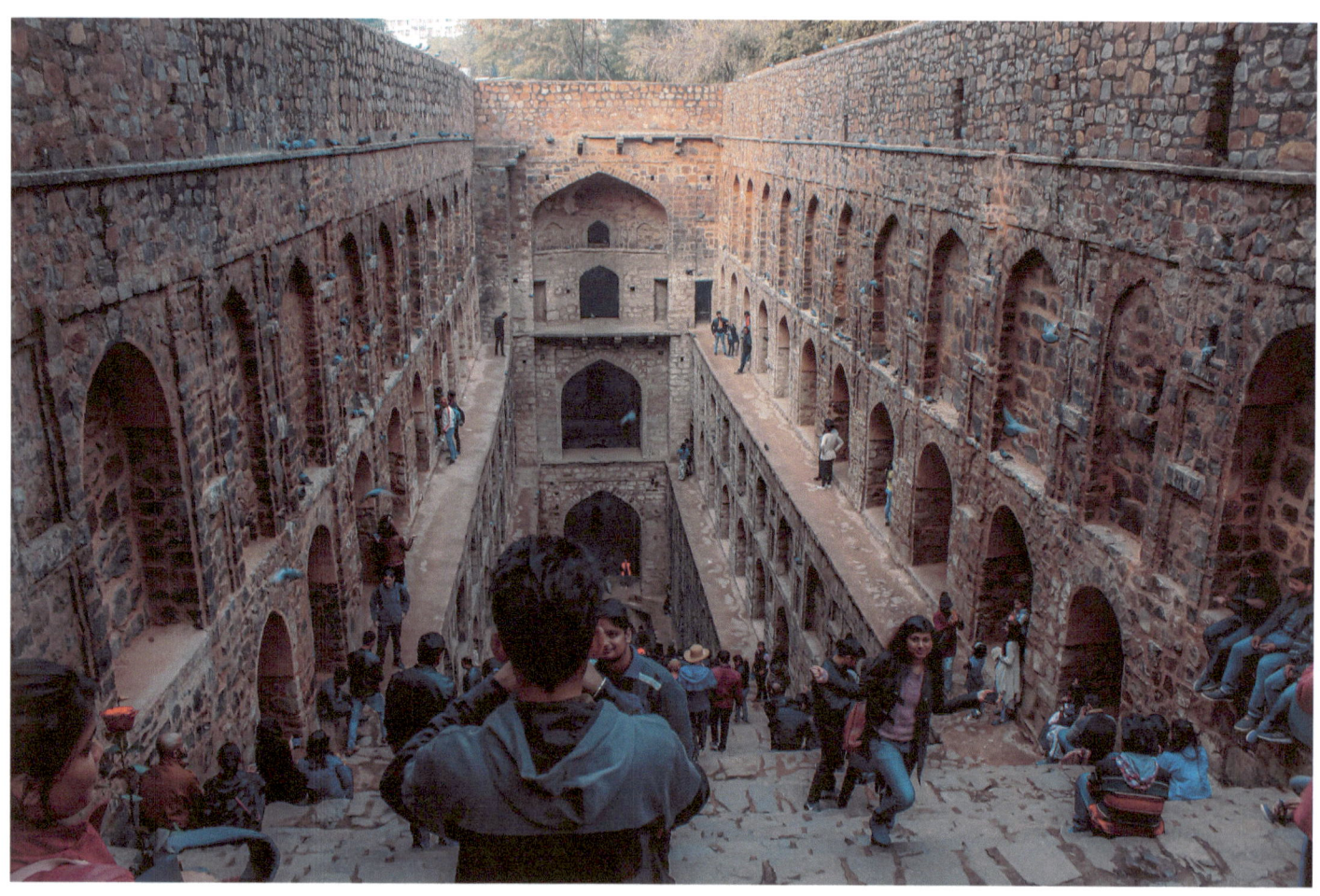

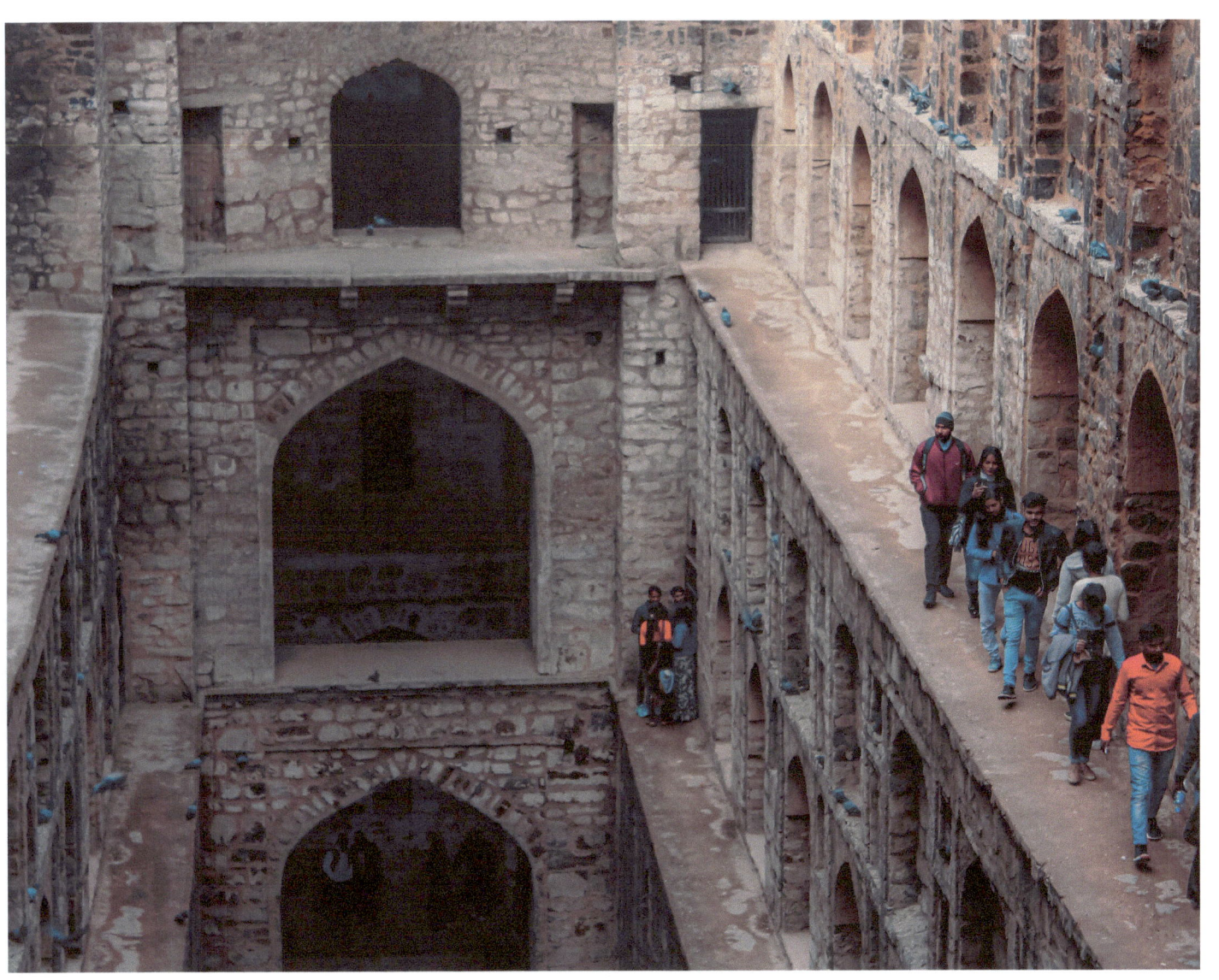

Eternal flame, India Gate...

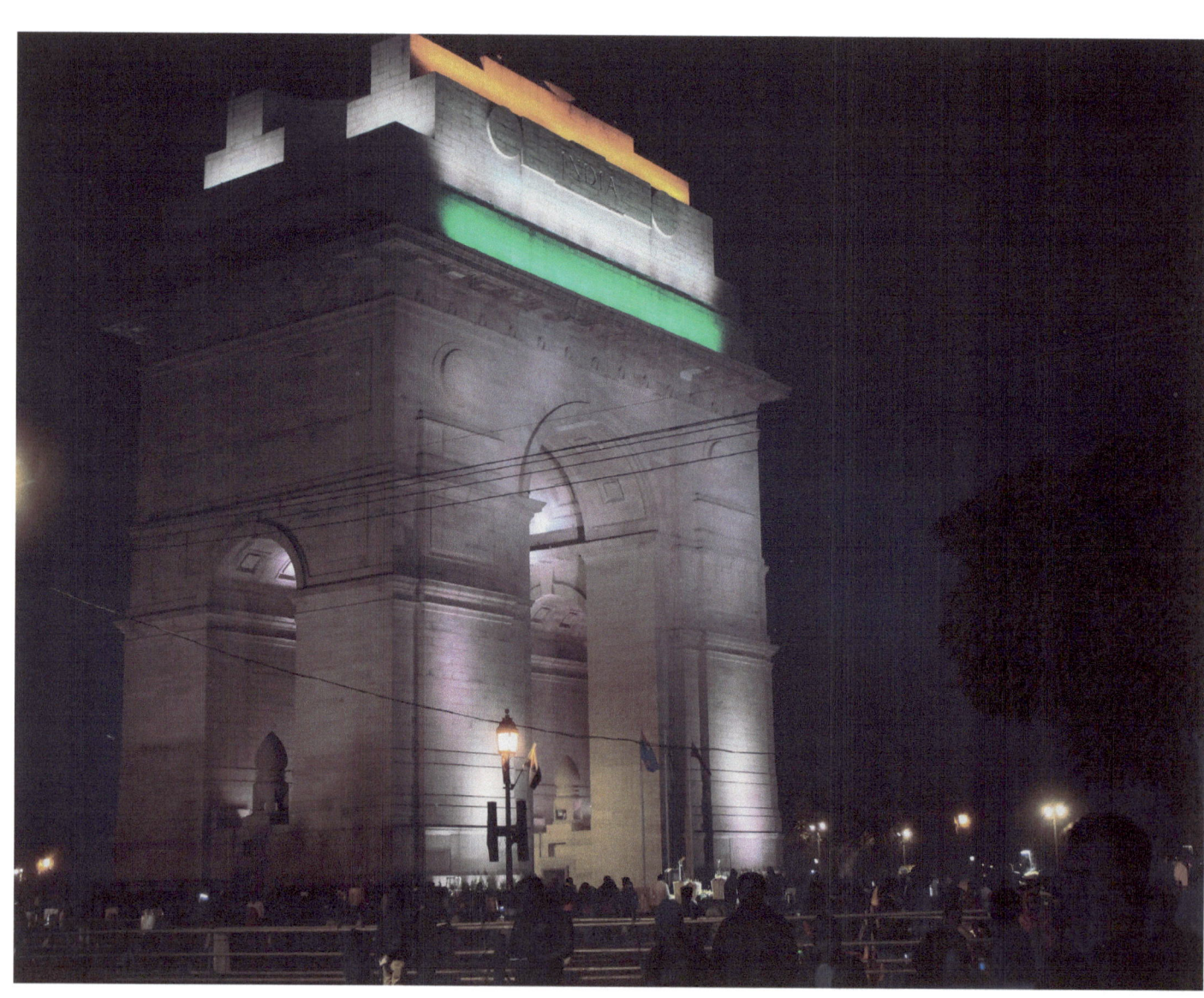

Noorpur village, in Deoband, Uttar Pradesh

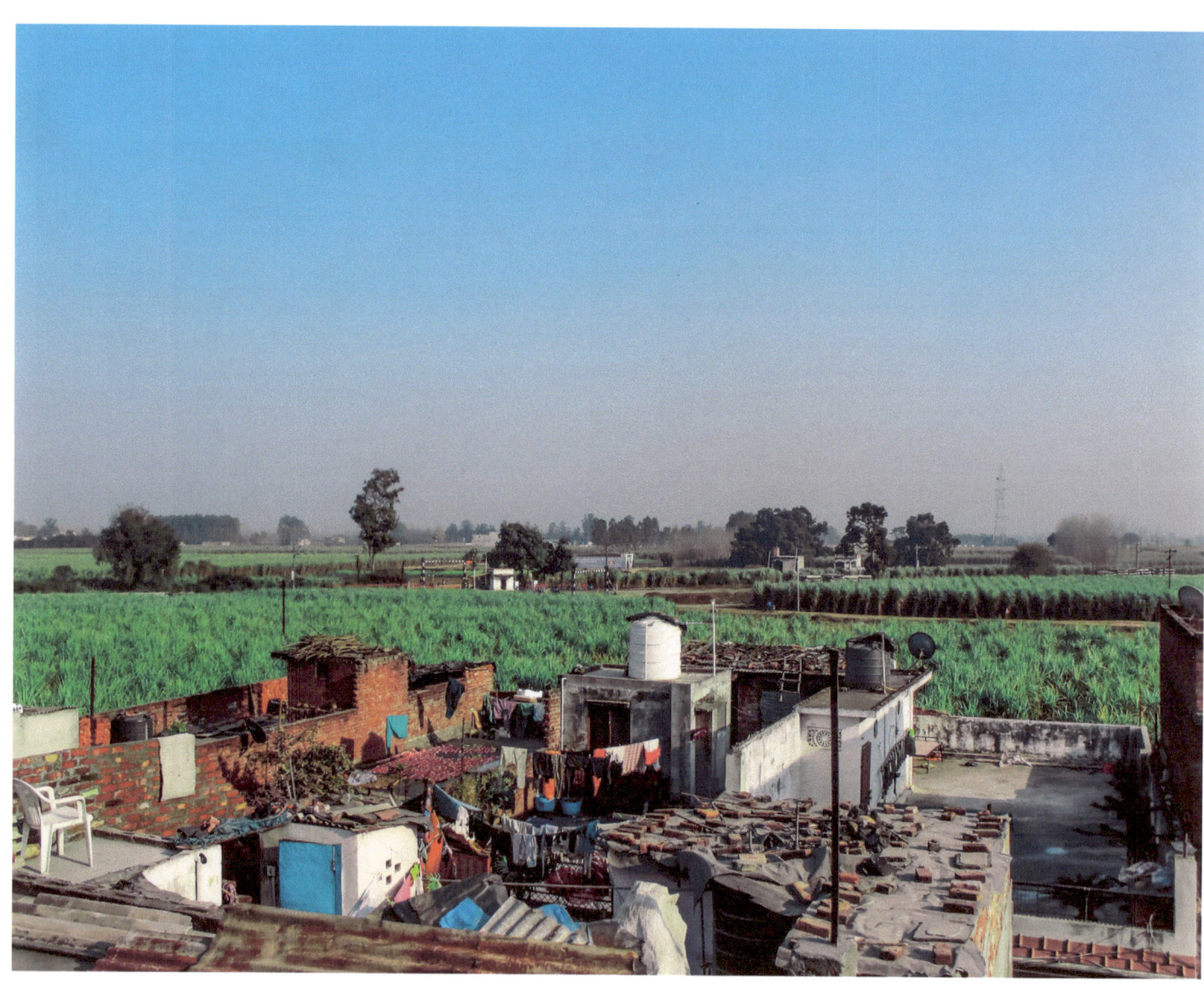

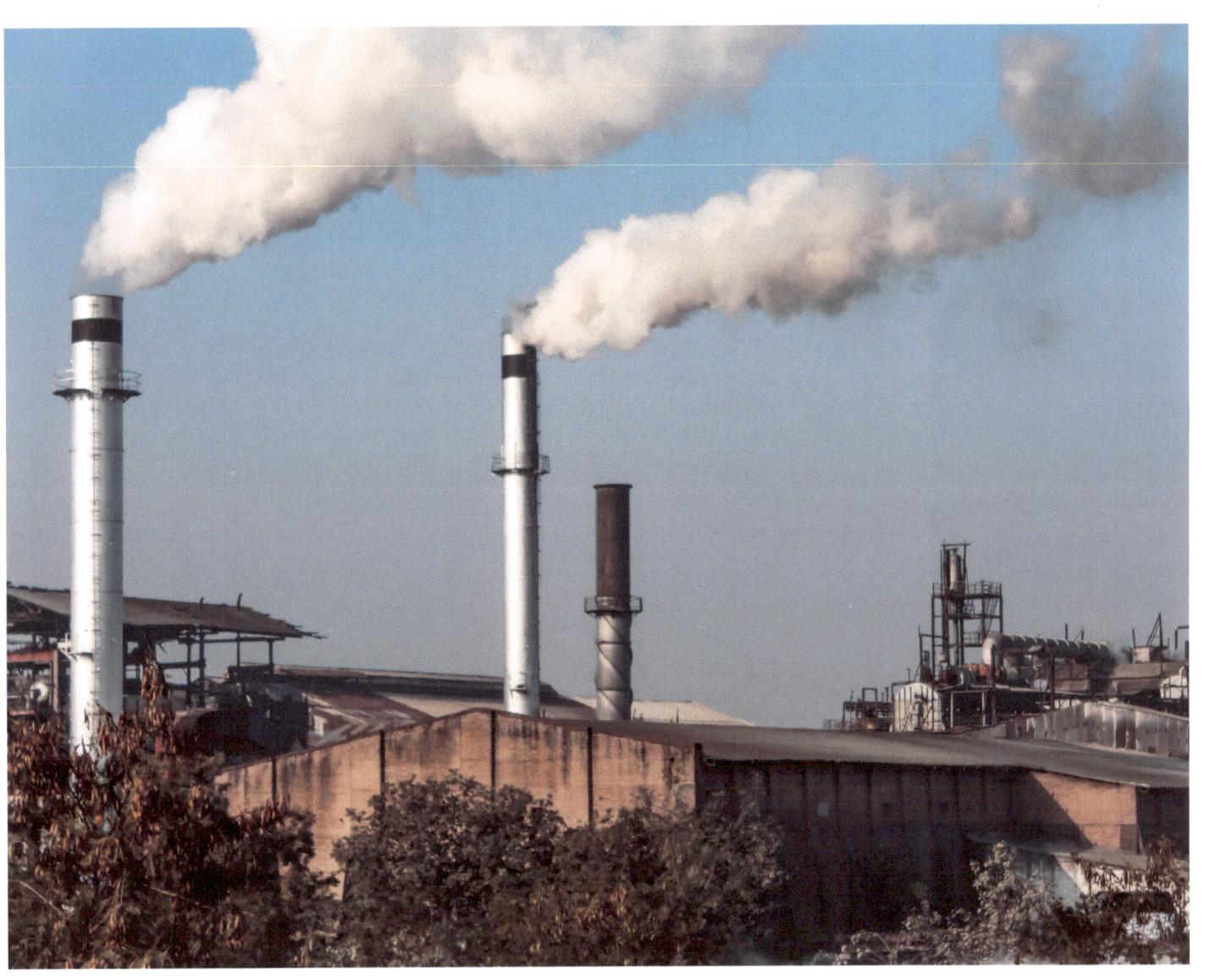

Enter the ancient city of Gujarat…

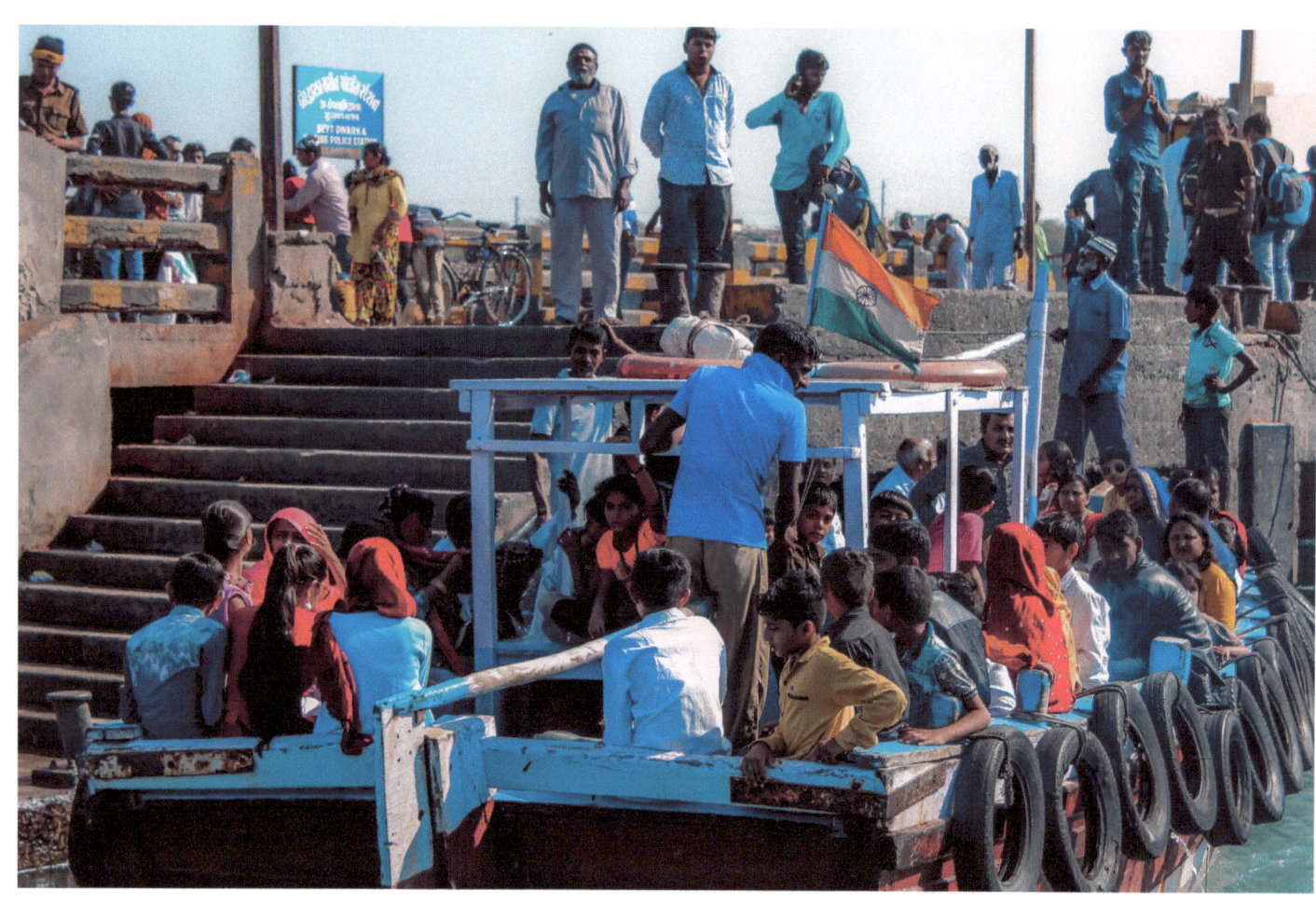

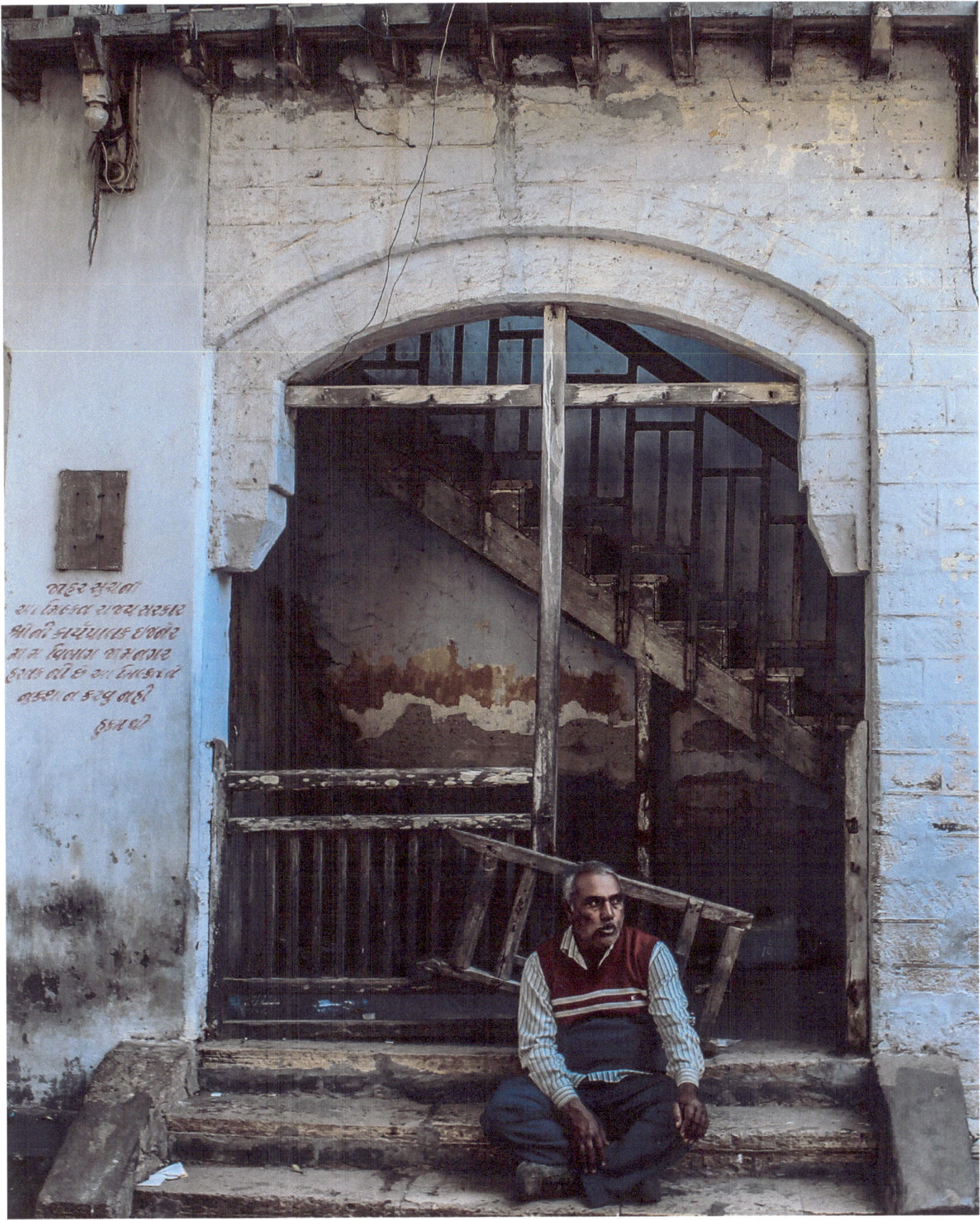

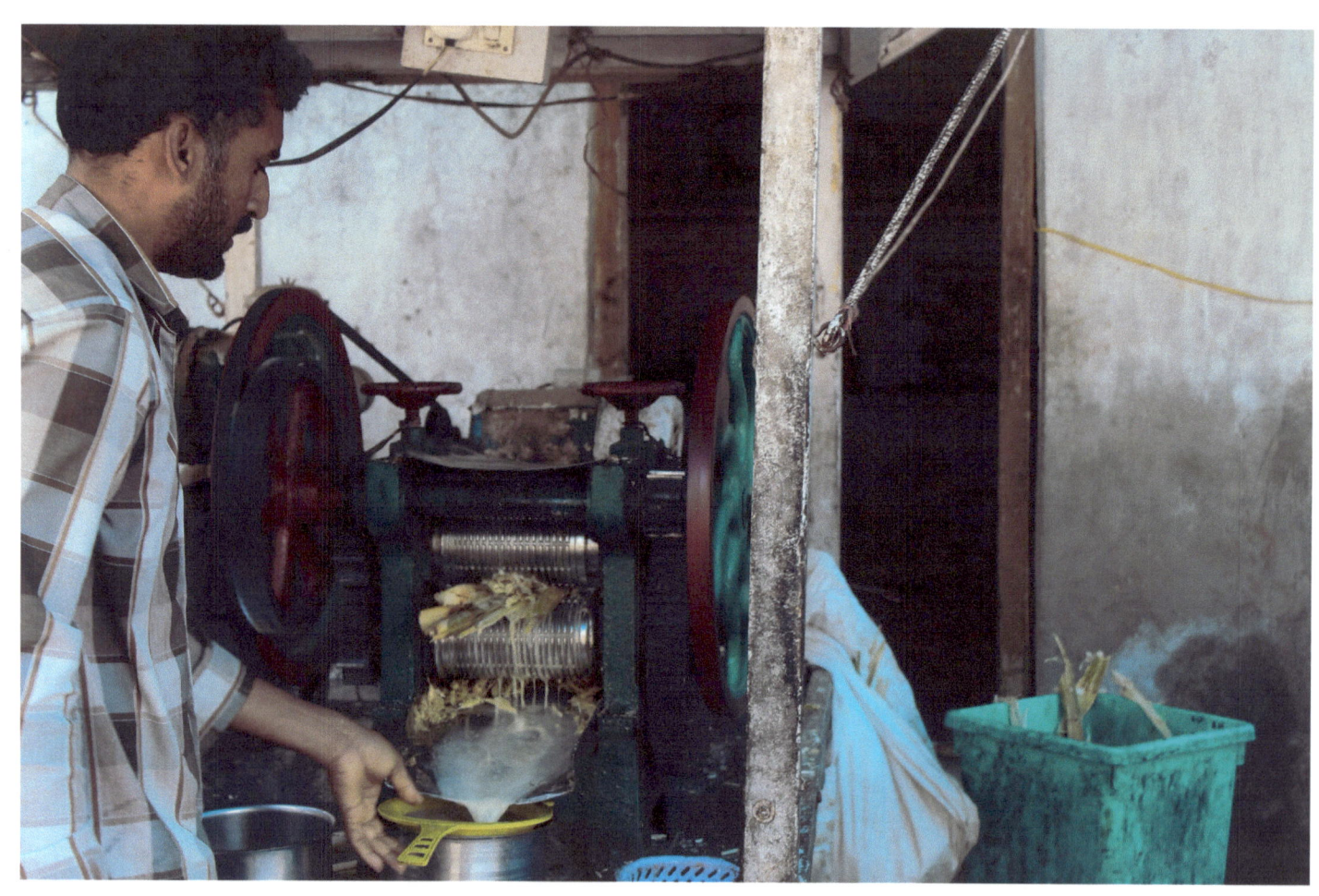

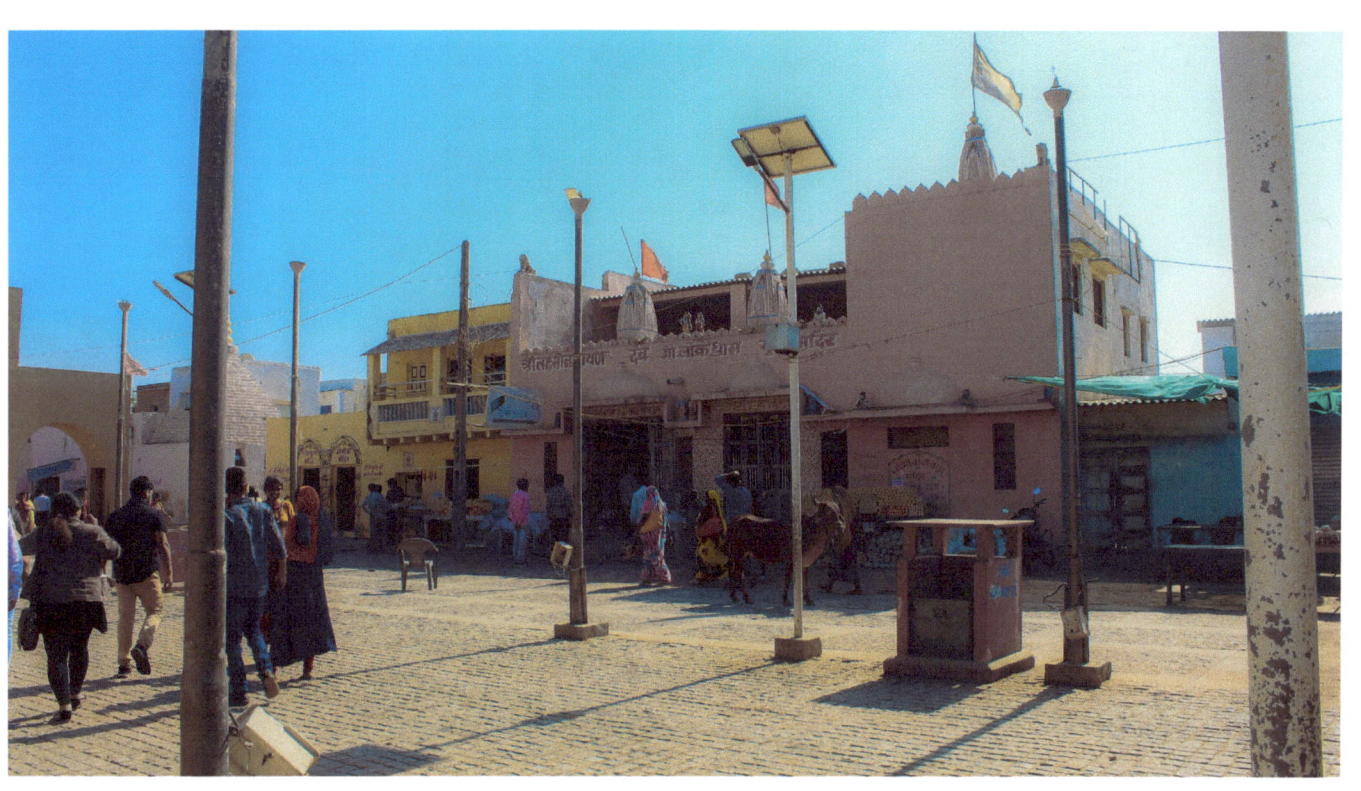

Colours of Beyt Dwarka...

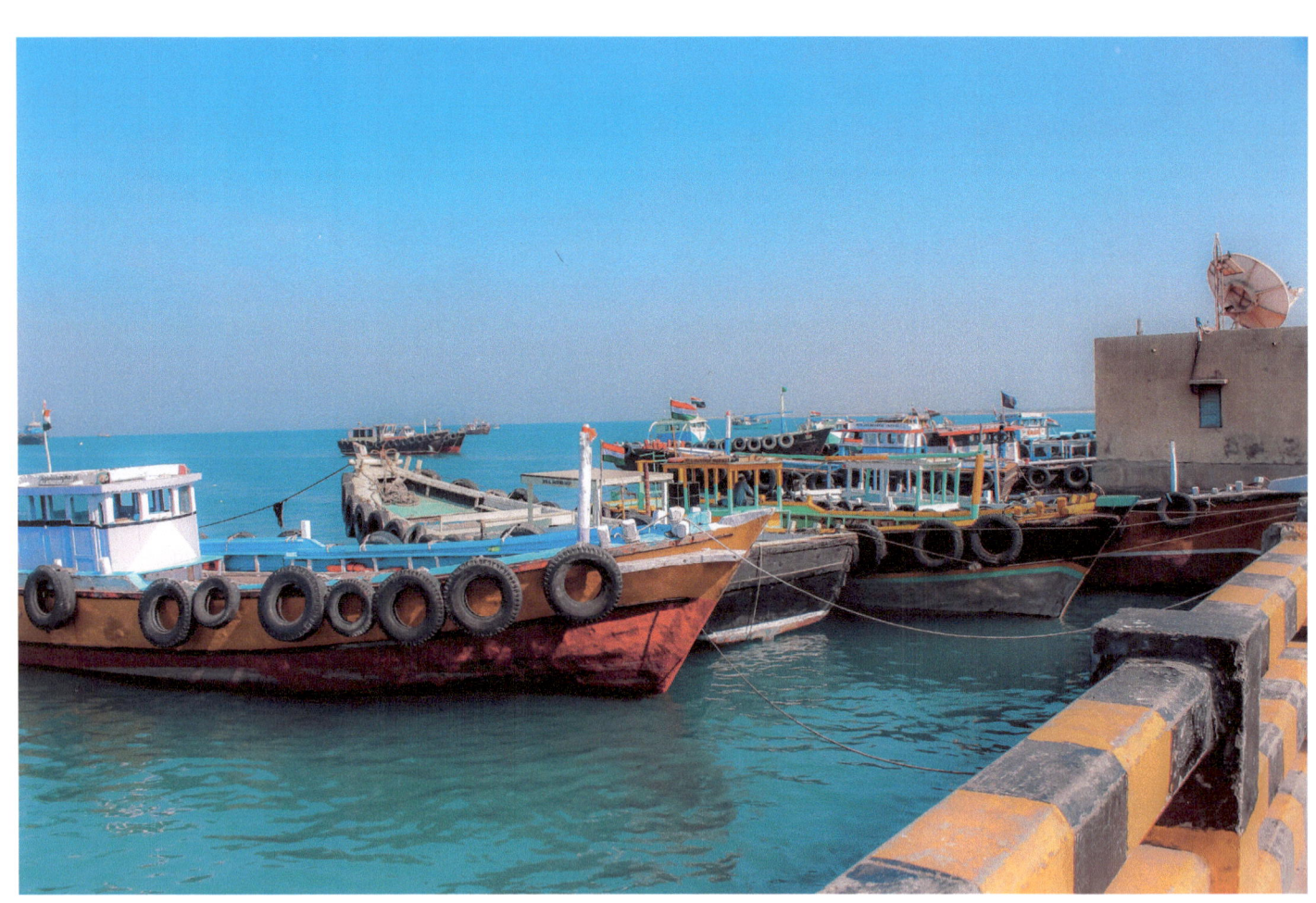

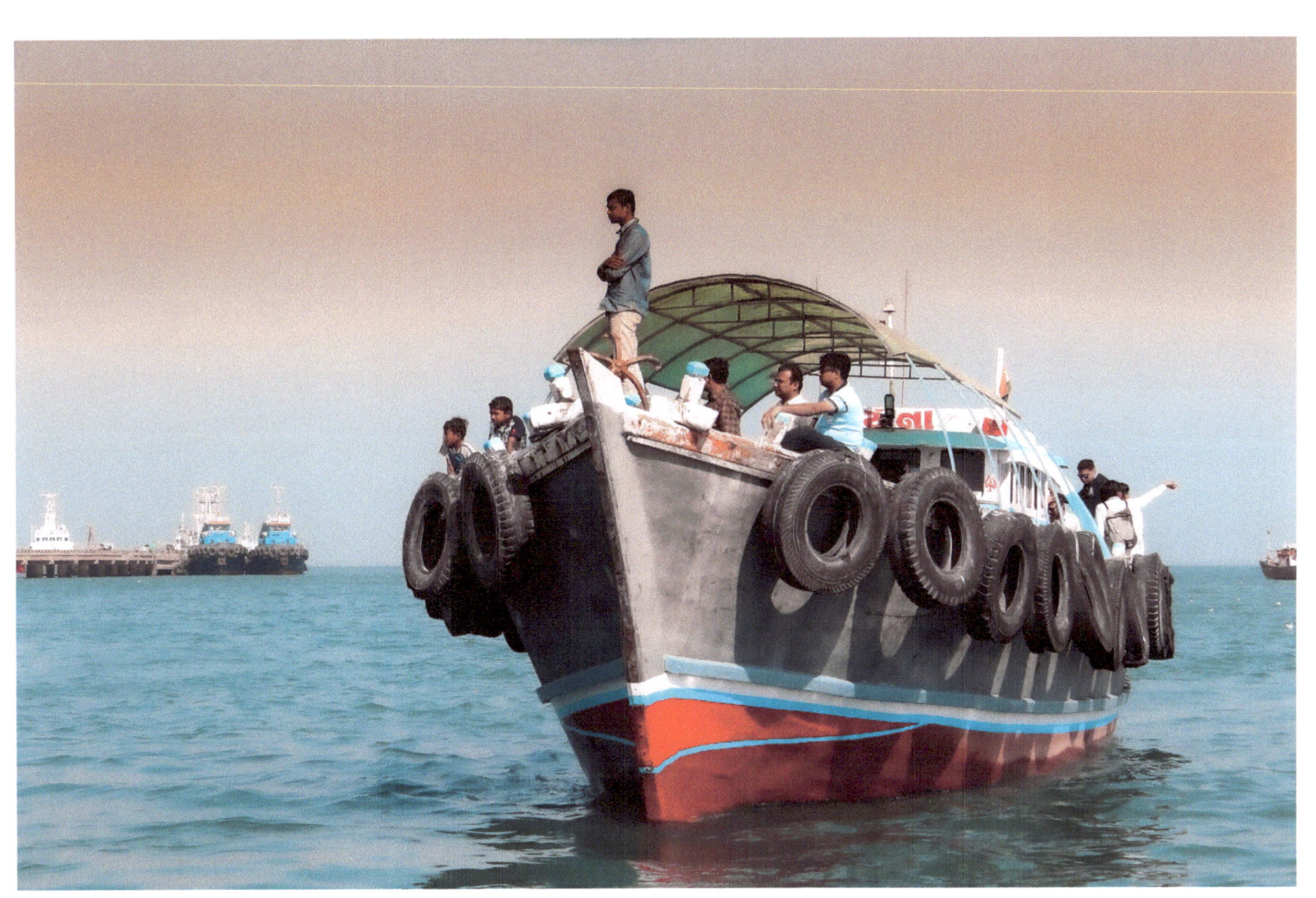

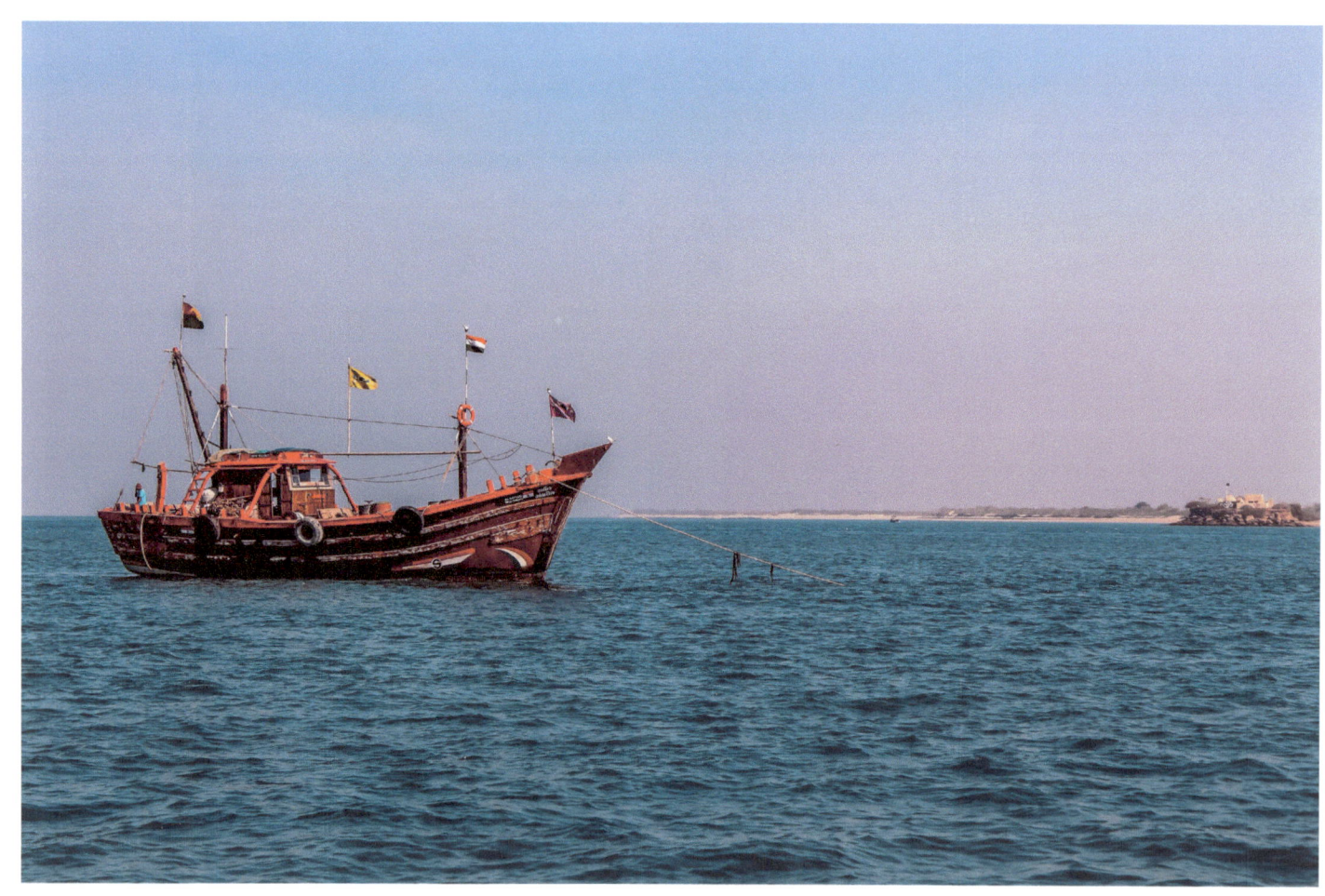

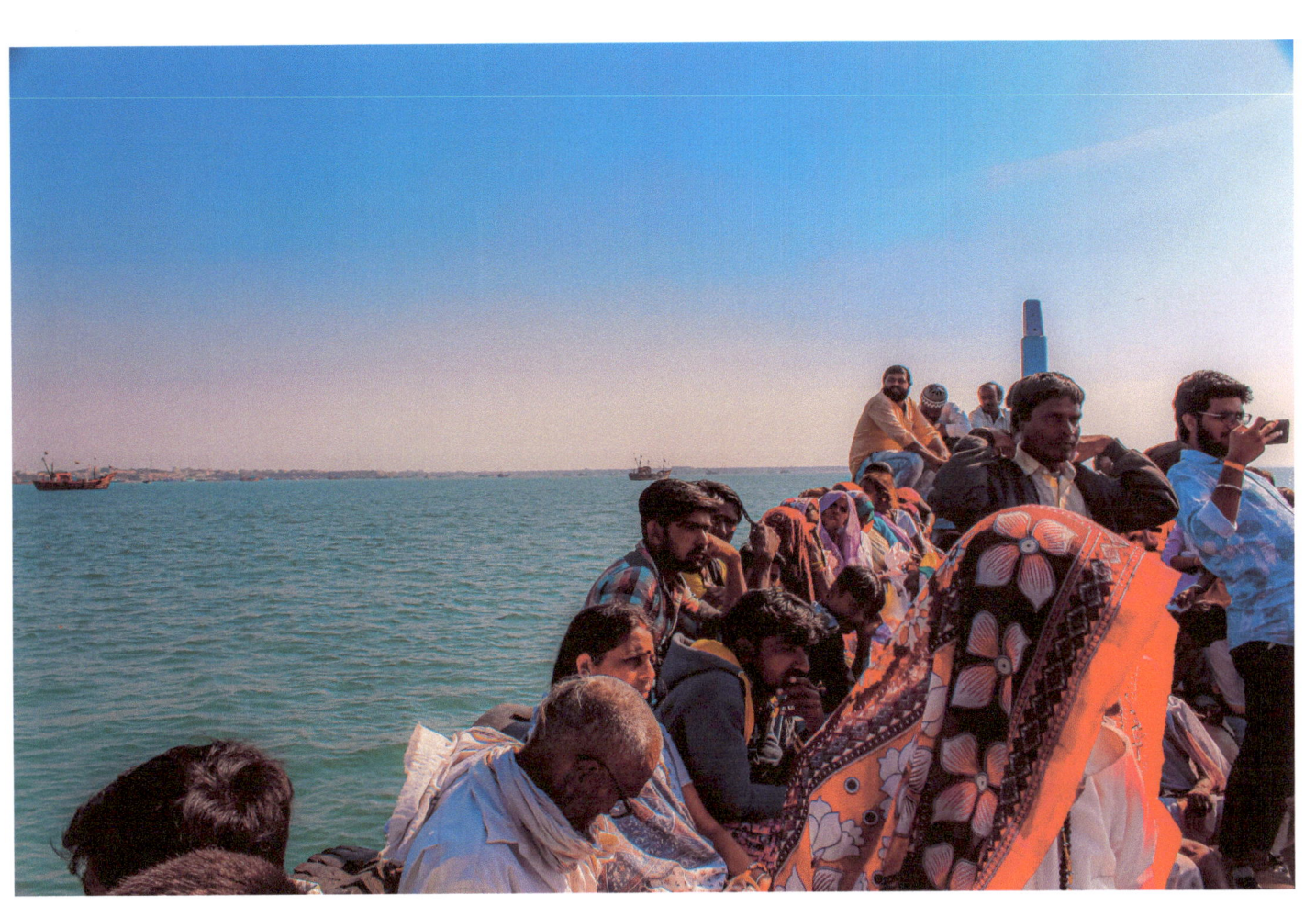

Portraits of few friendly strangers, on the shores of Beyt Dwarka...

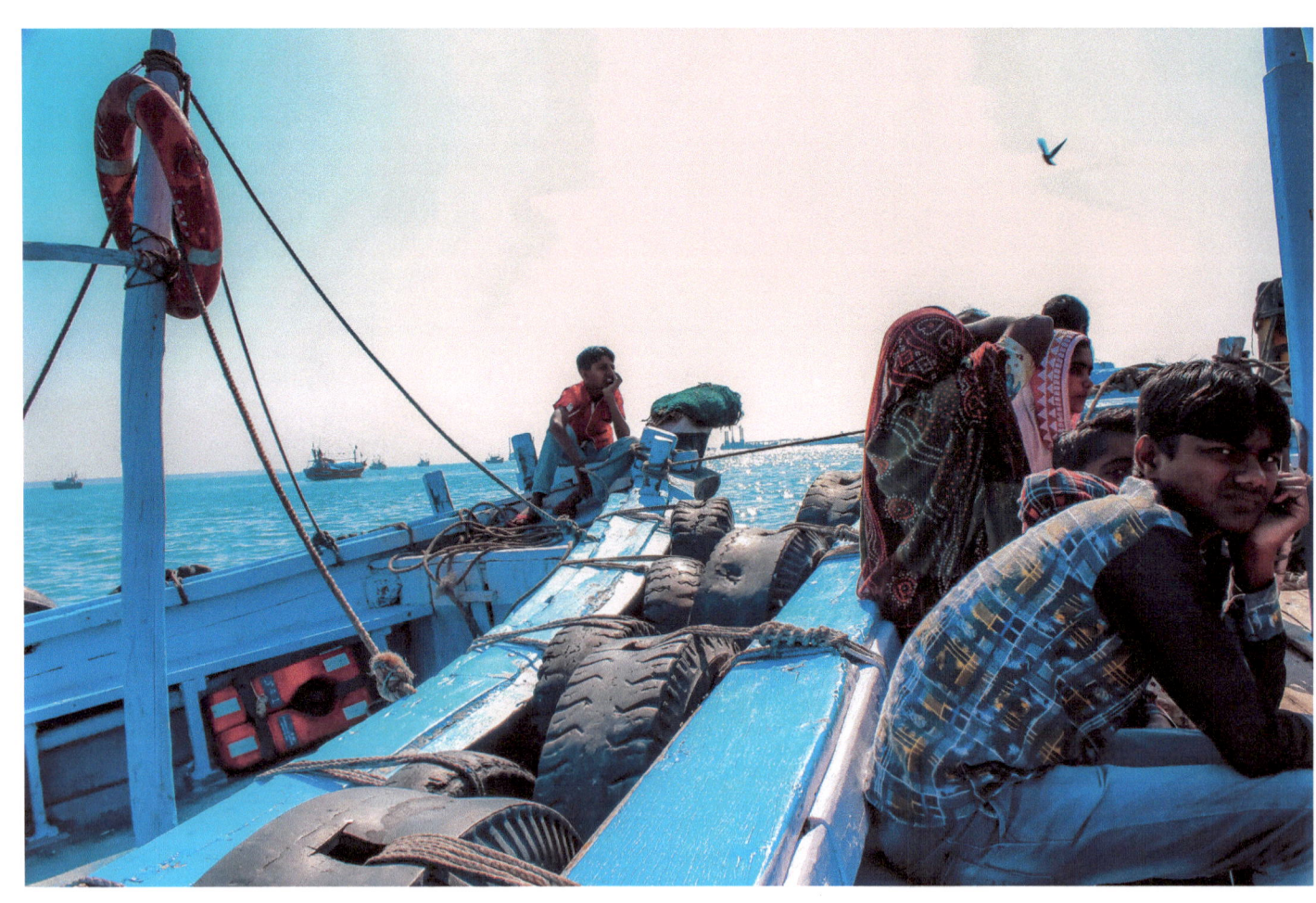

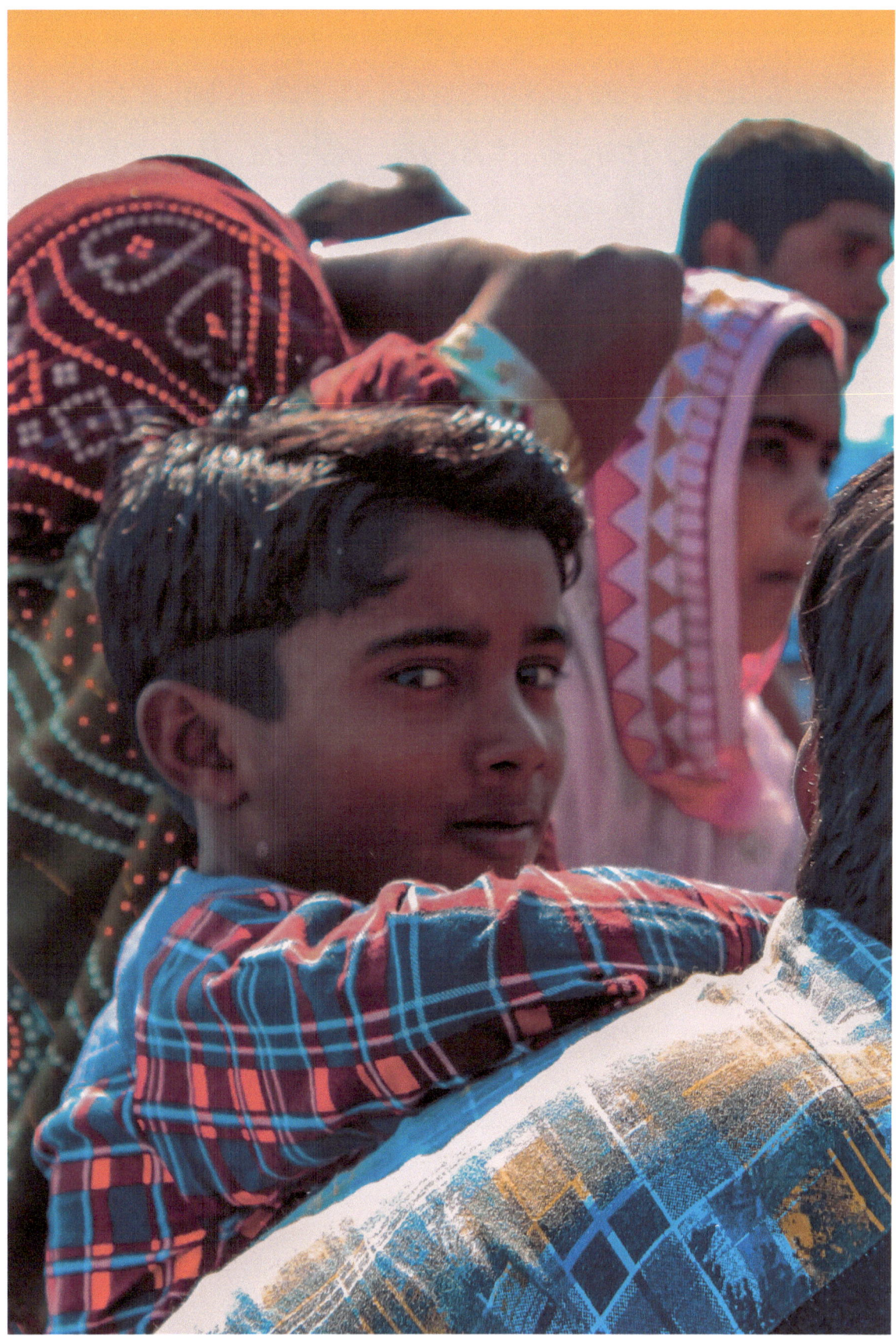

These locals requested me to photograph them while I was traveling on the local ferry to the Beyt Dwarka temple...

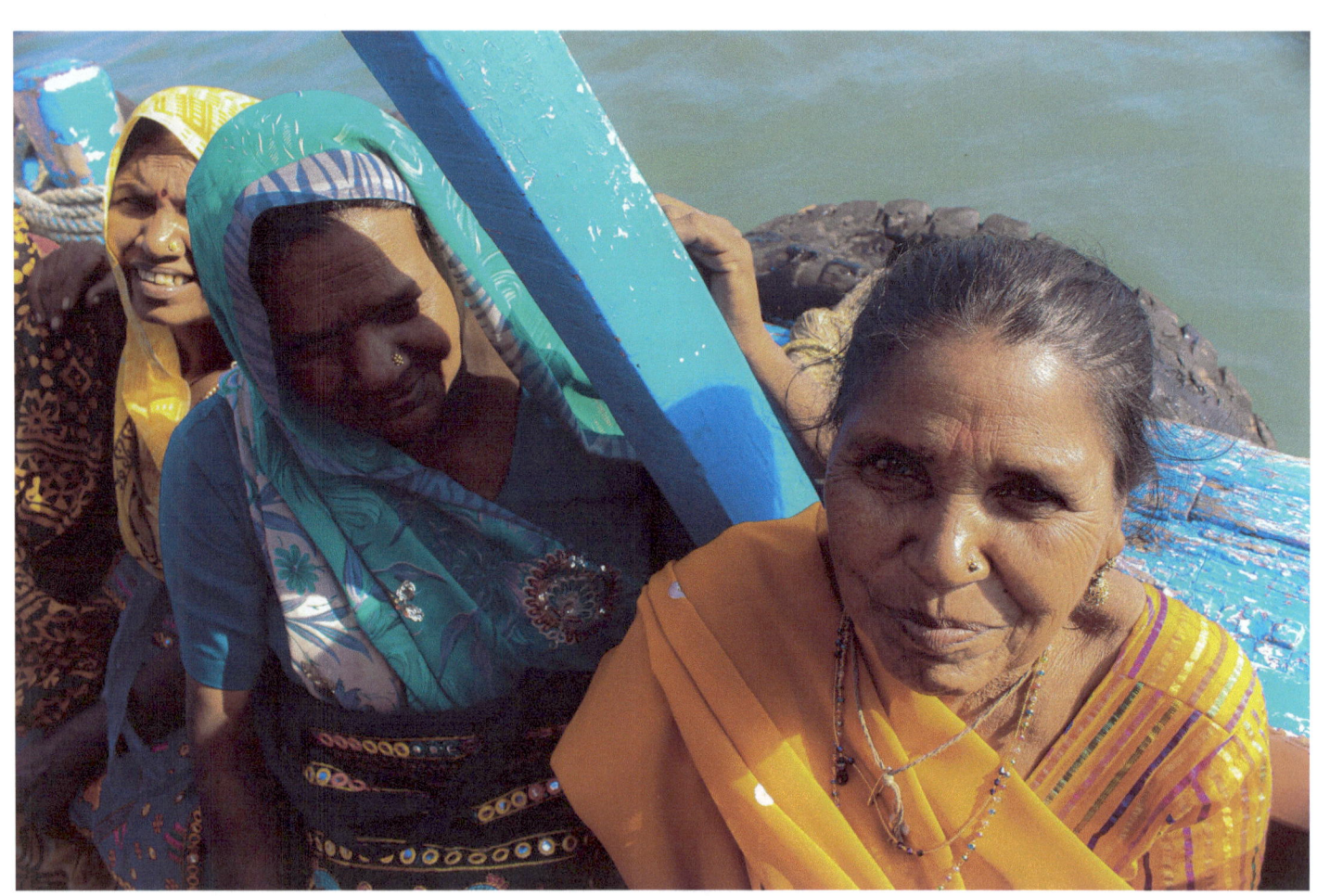

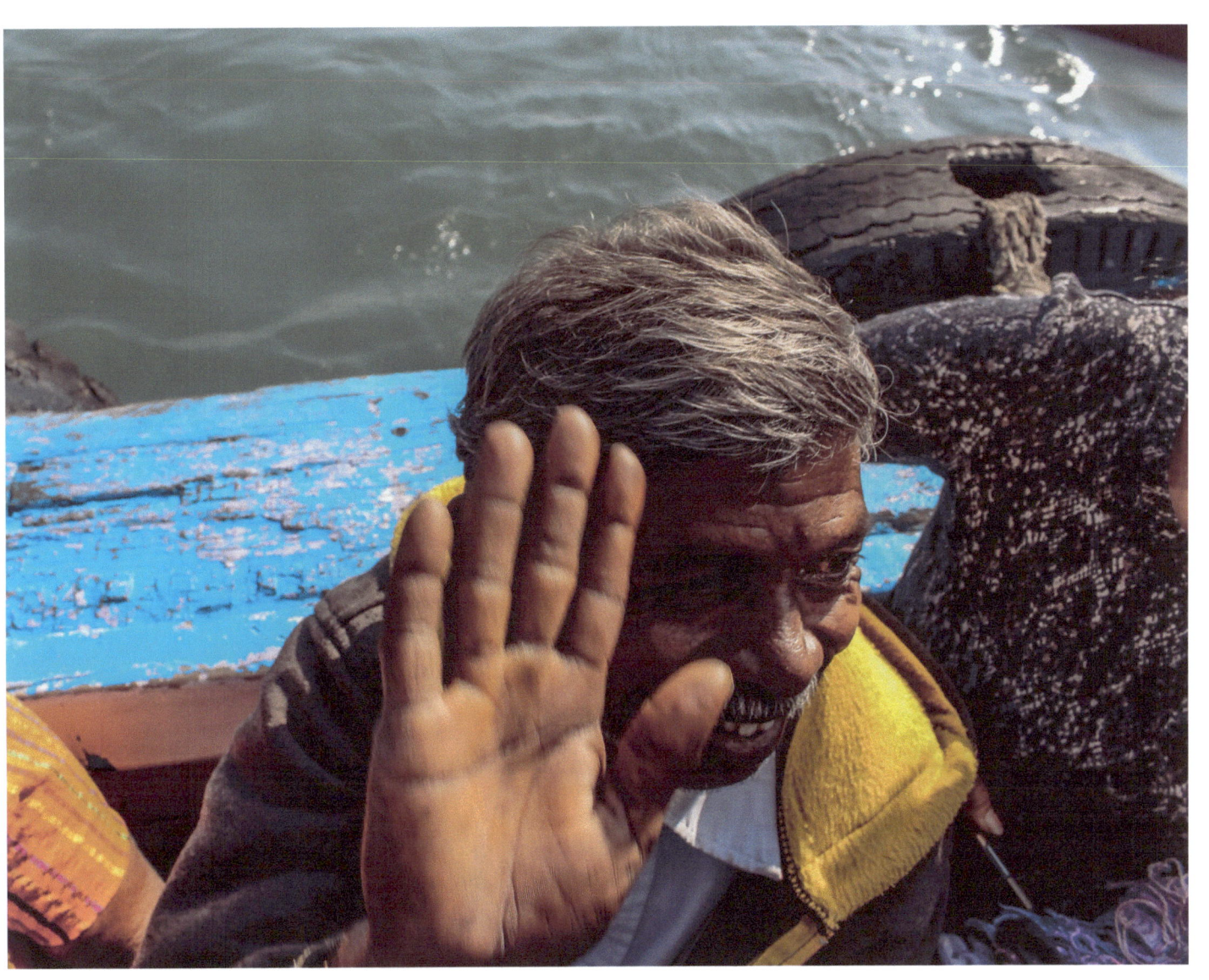

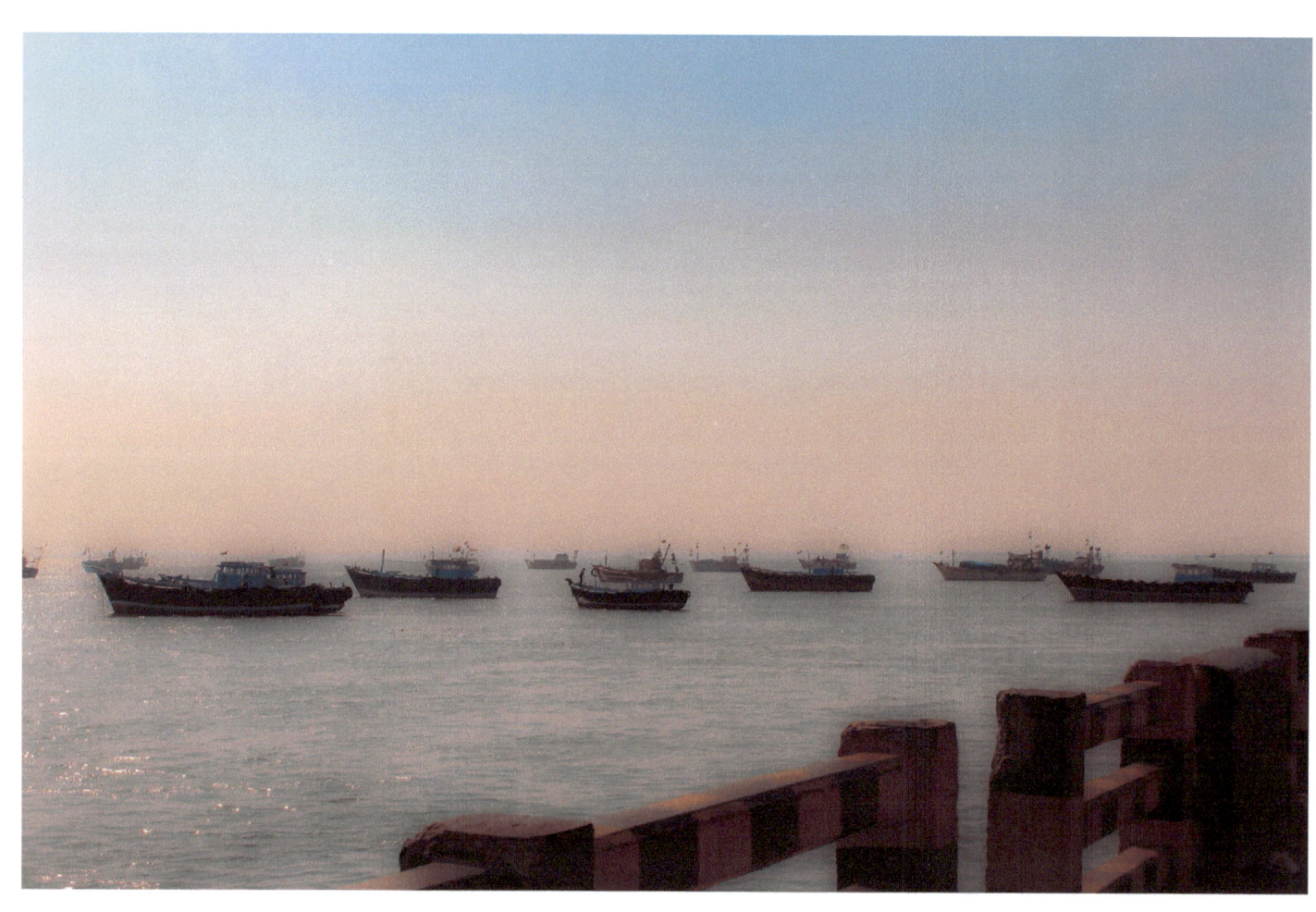

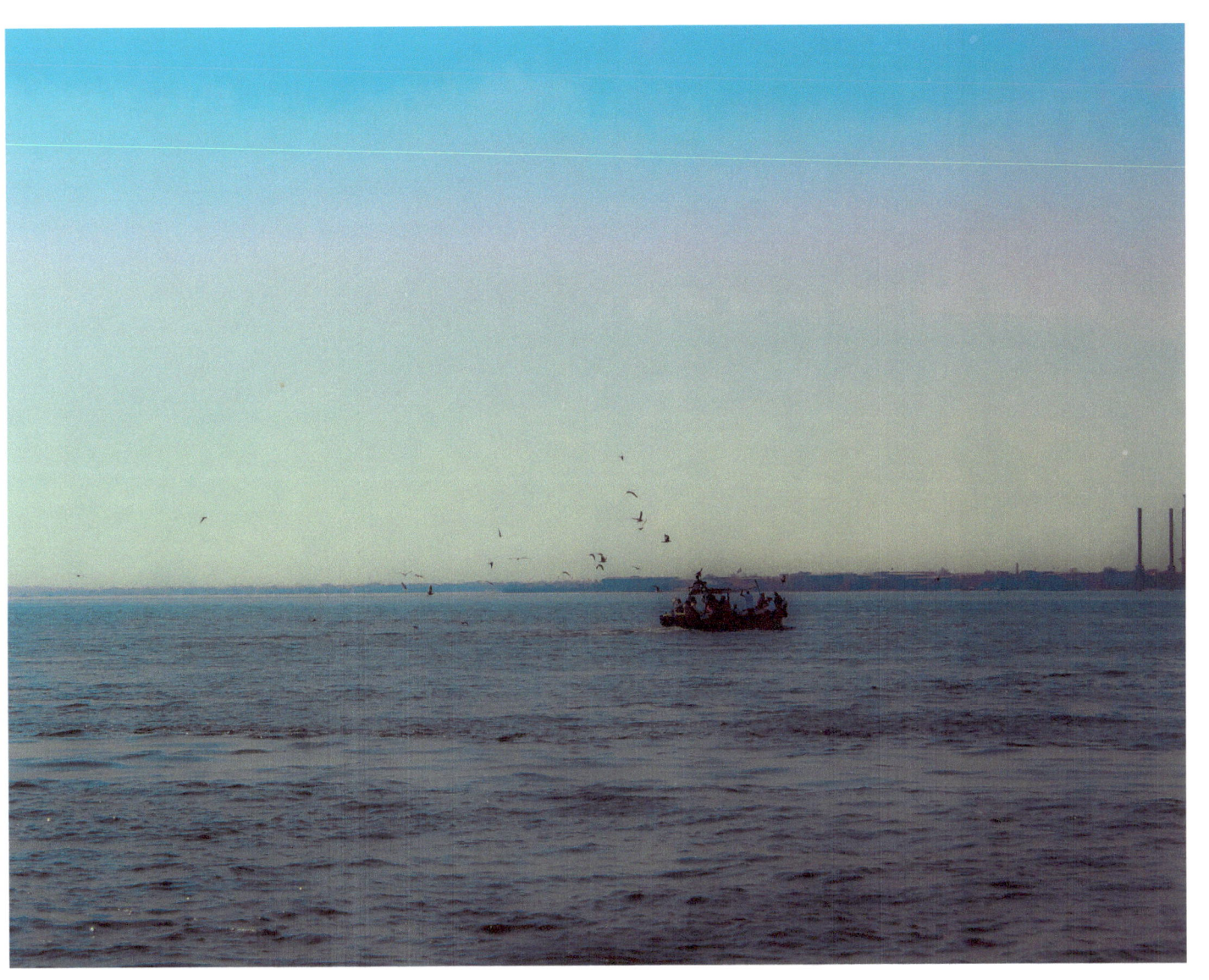

Holy Cows…

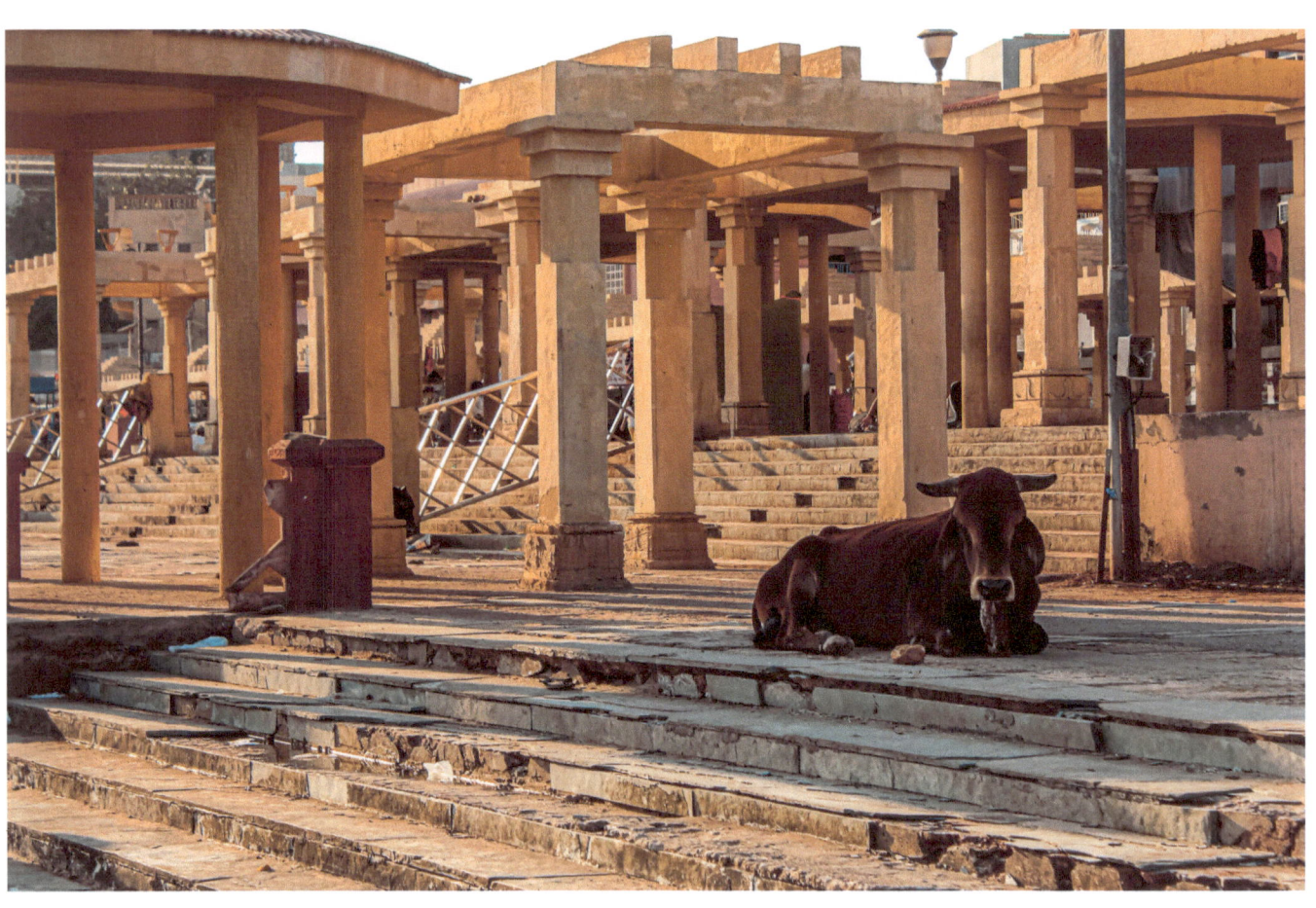

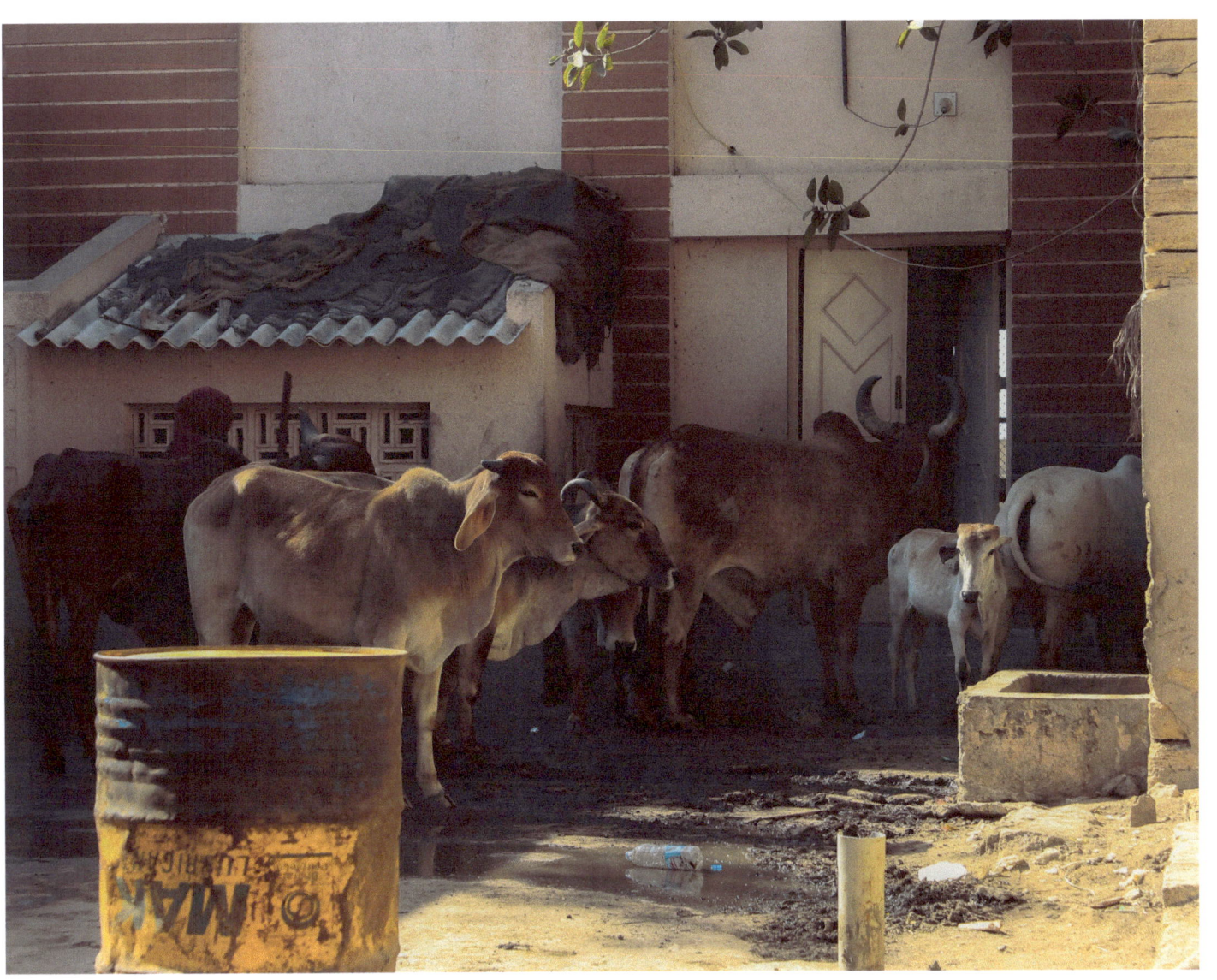

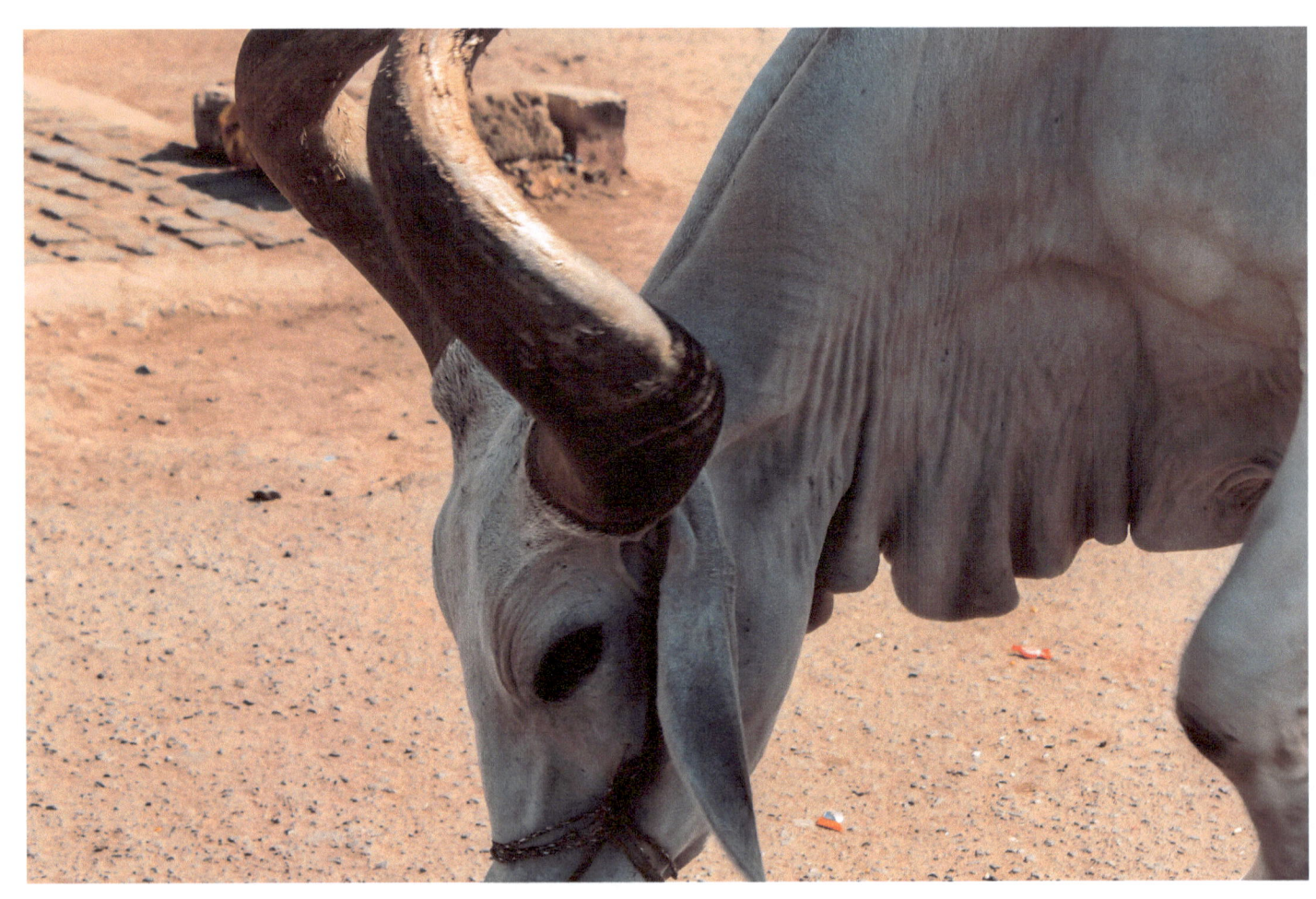

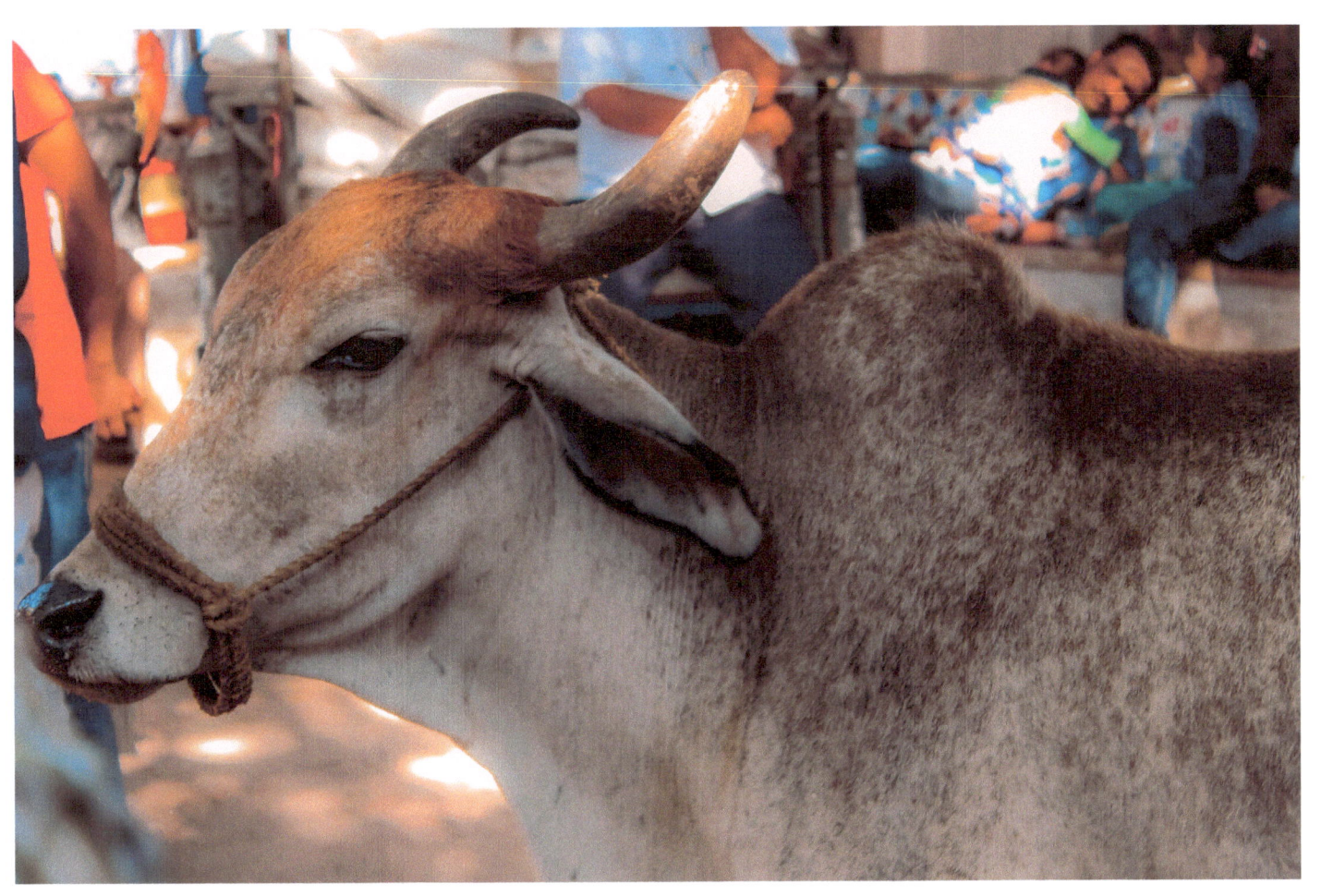

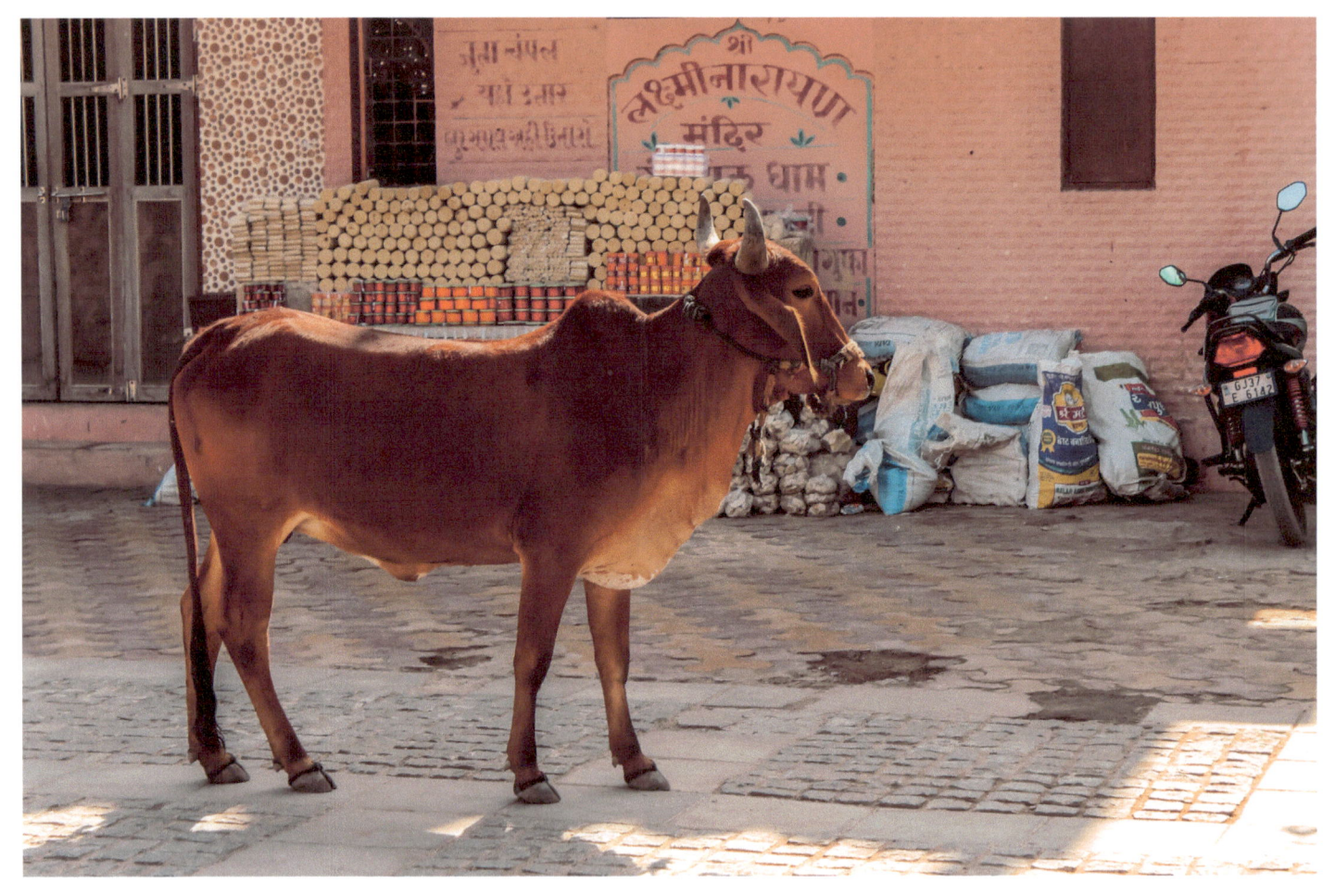

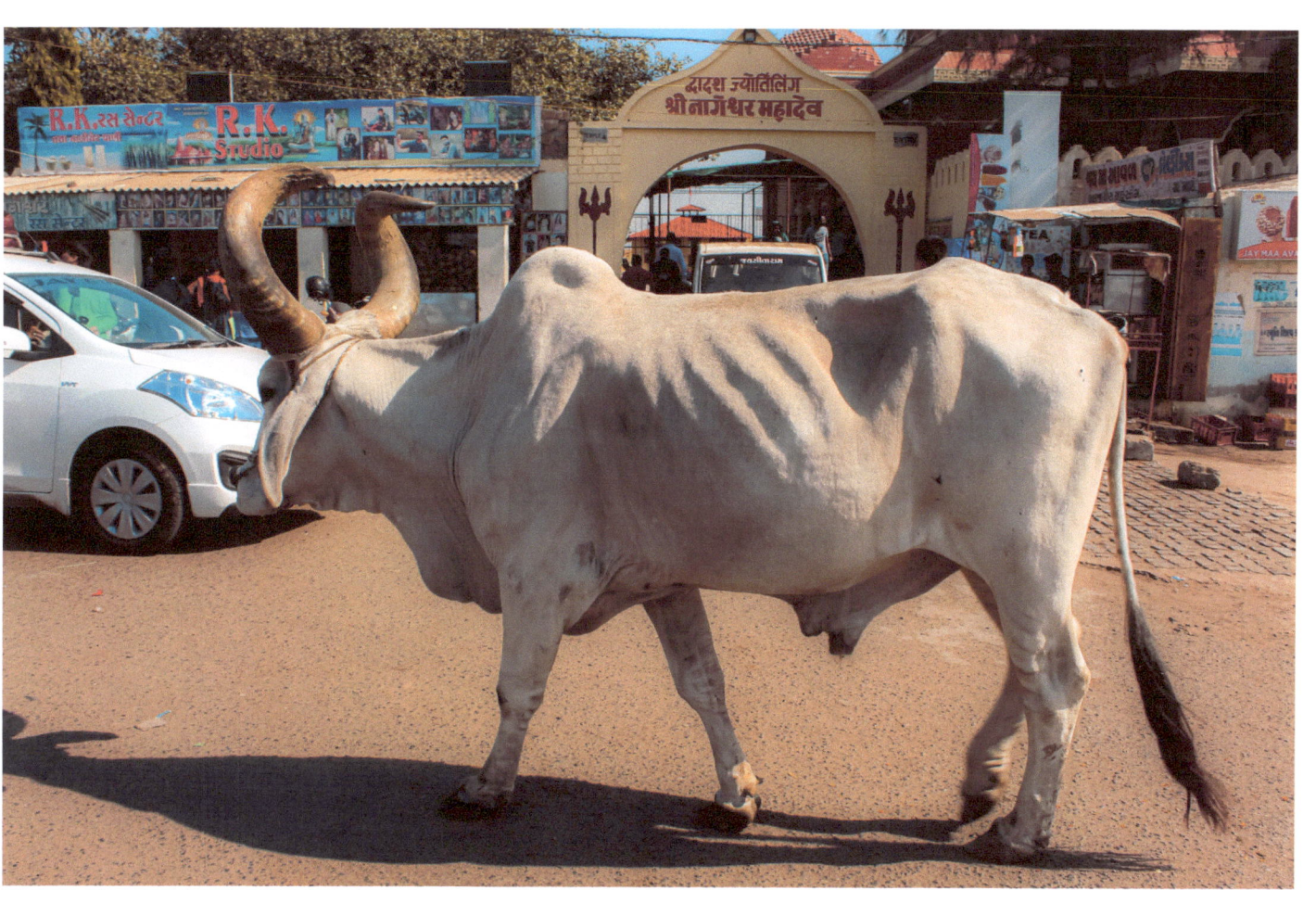

trolling on the ancient streets...

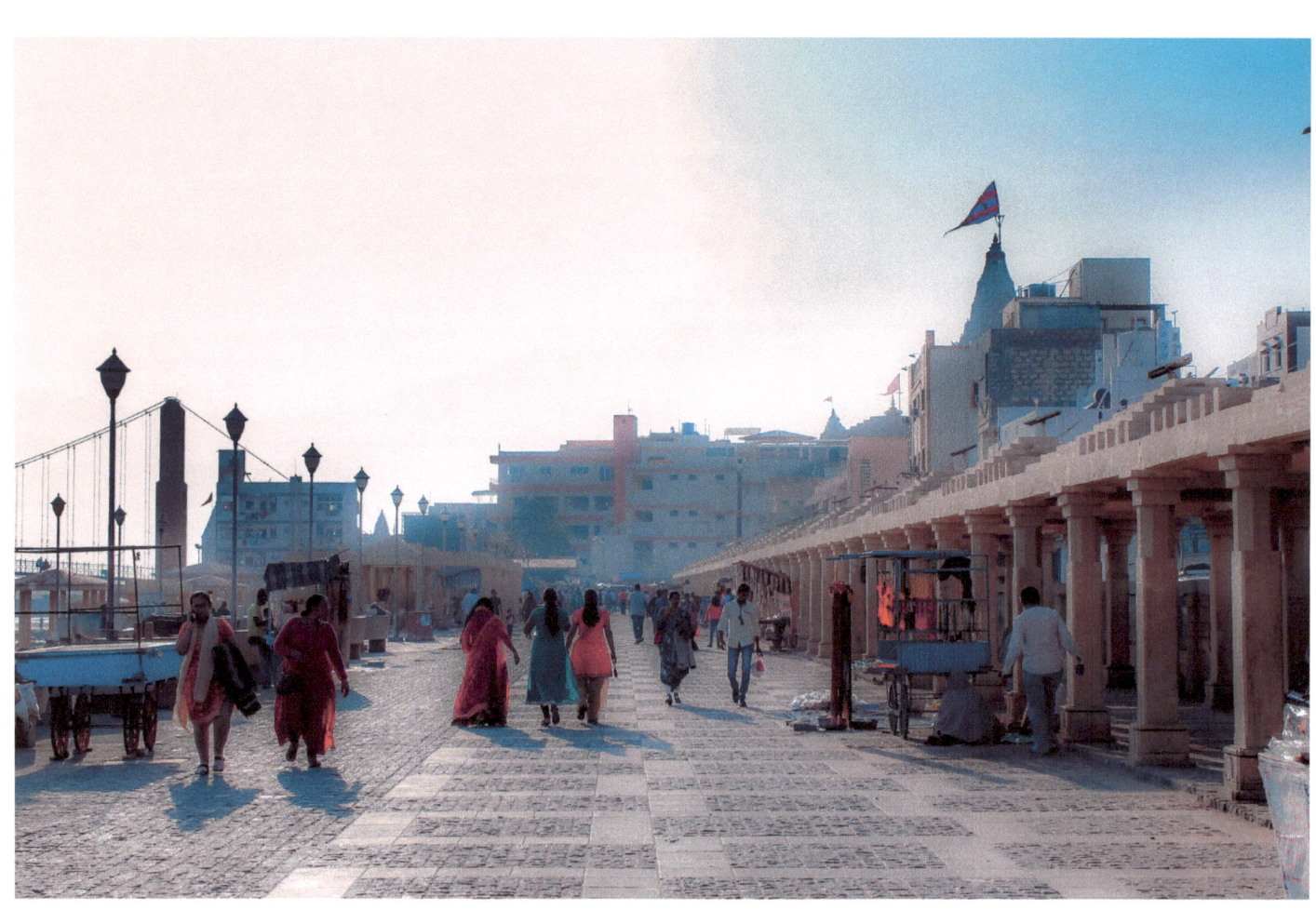

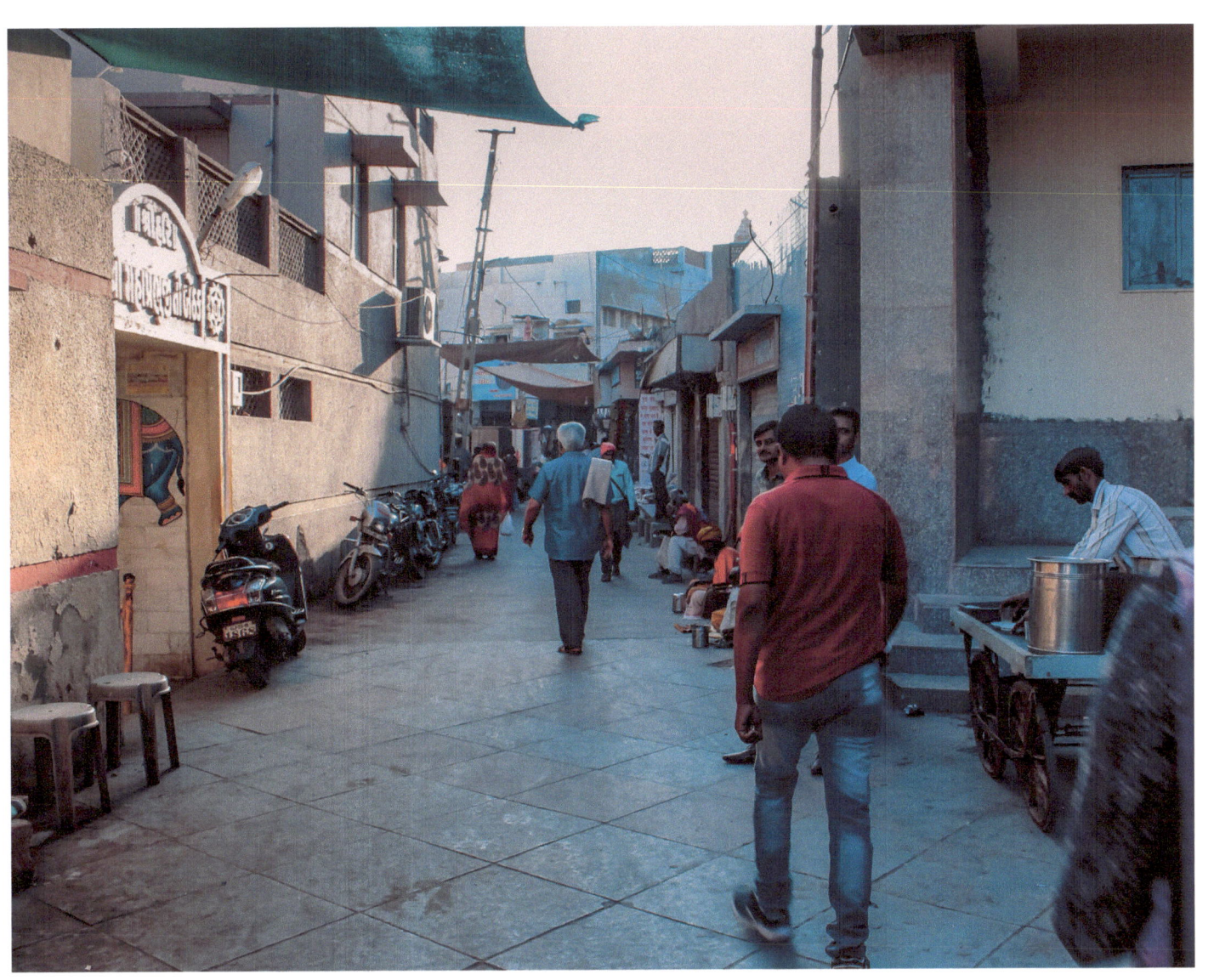

Dwarkadhish temple...

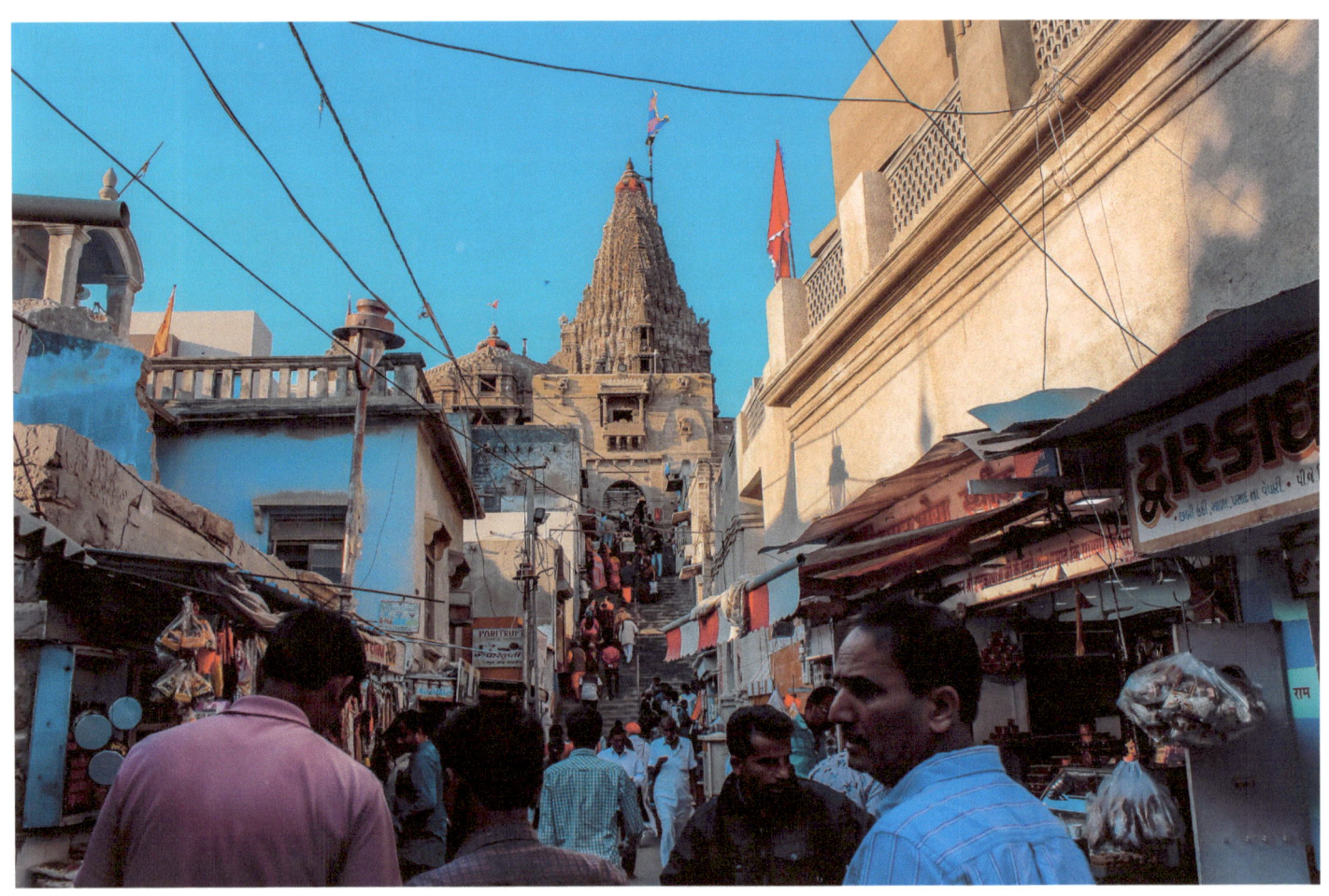

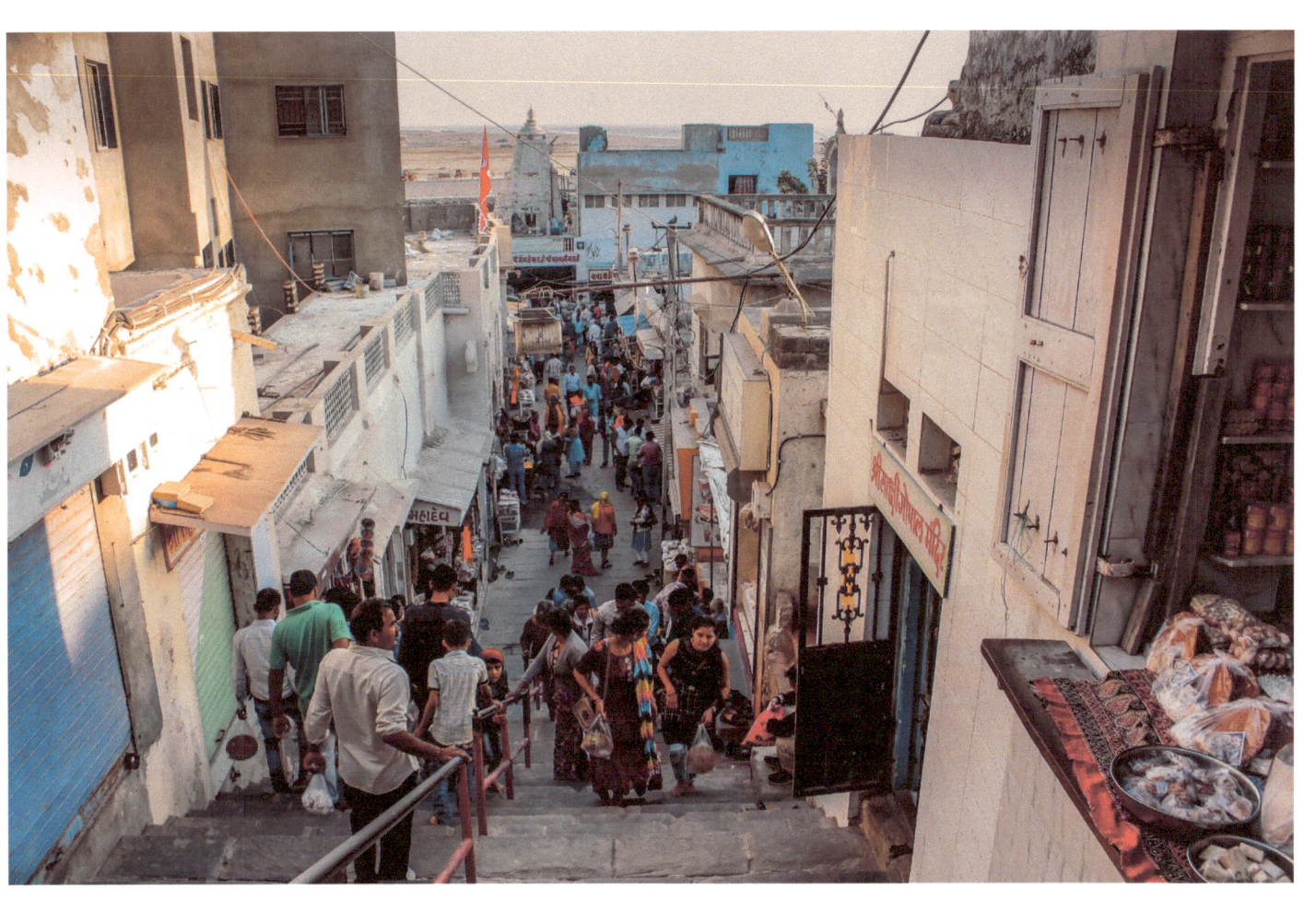

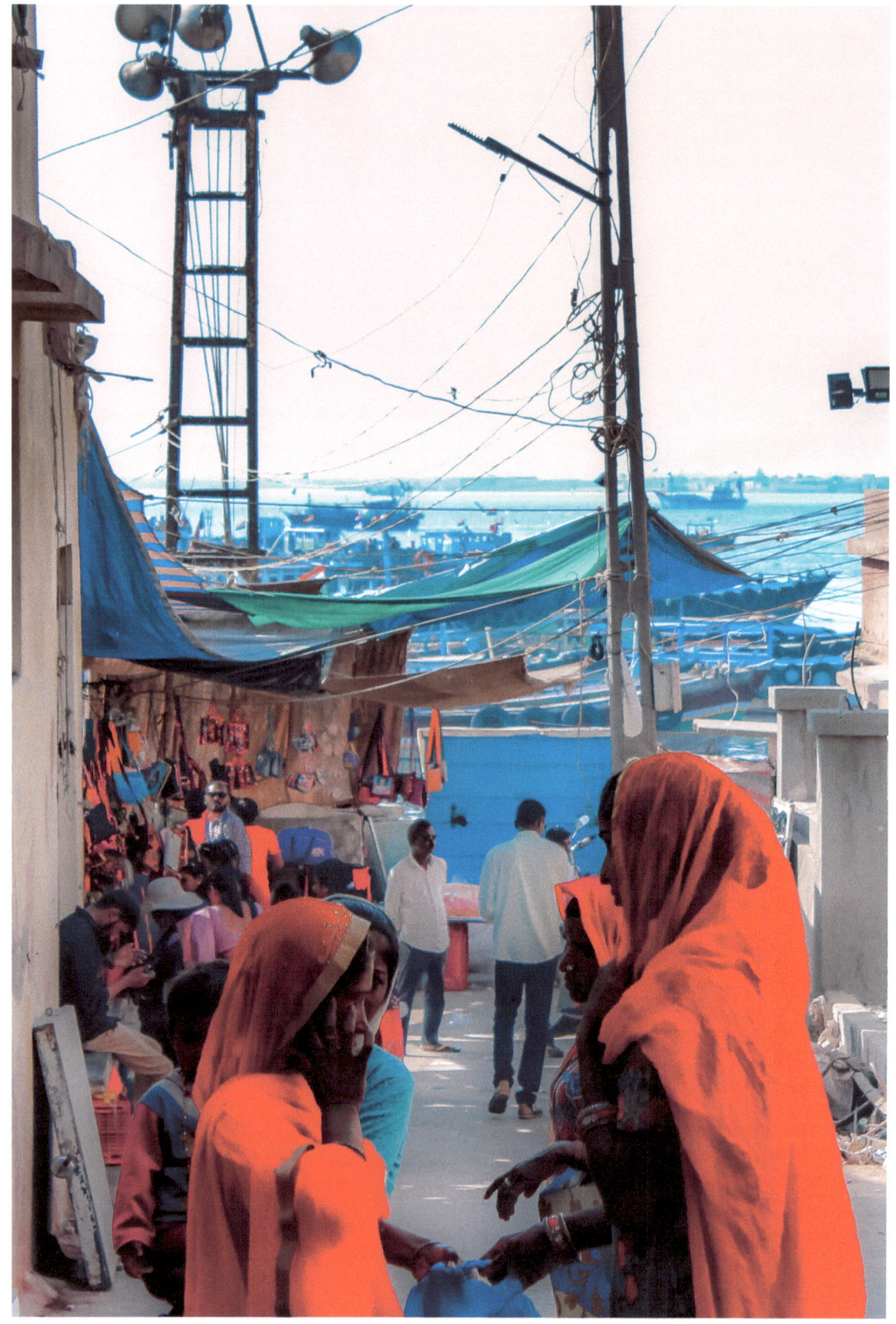

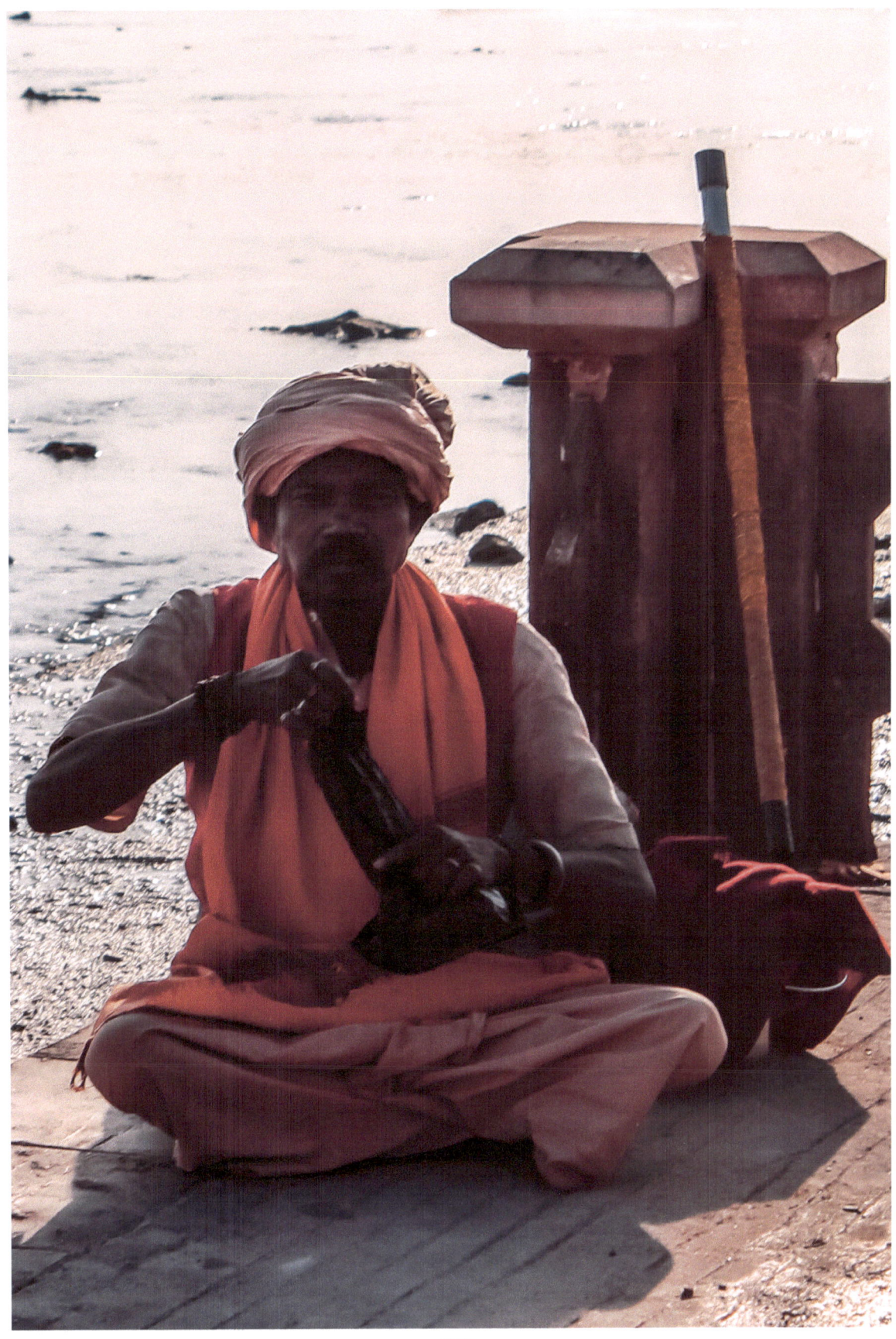

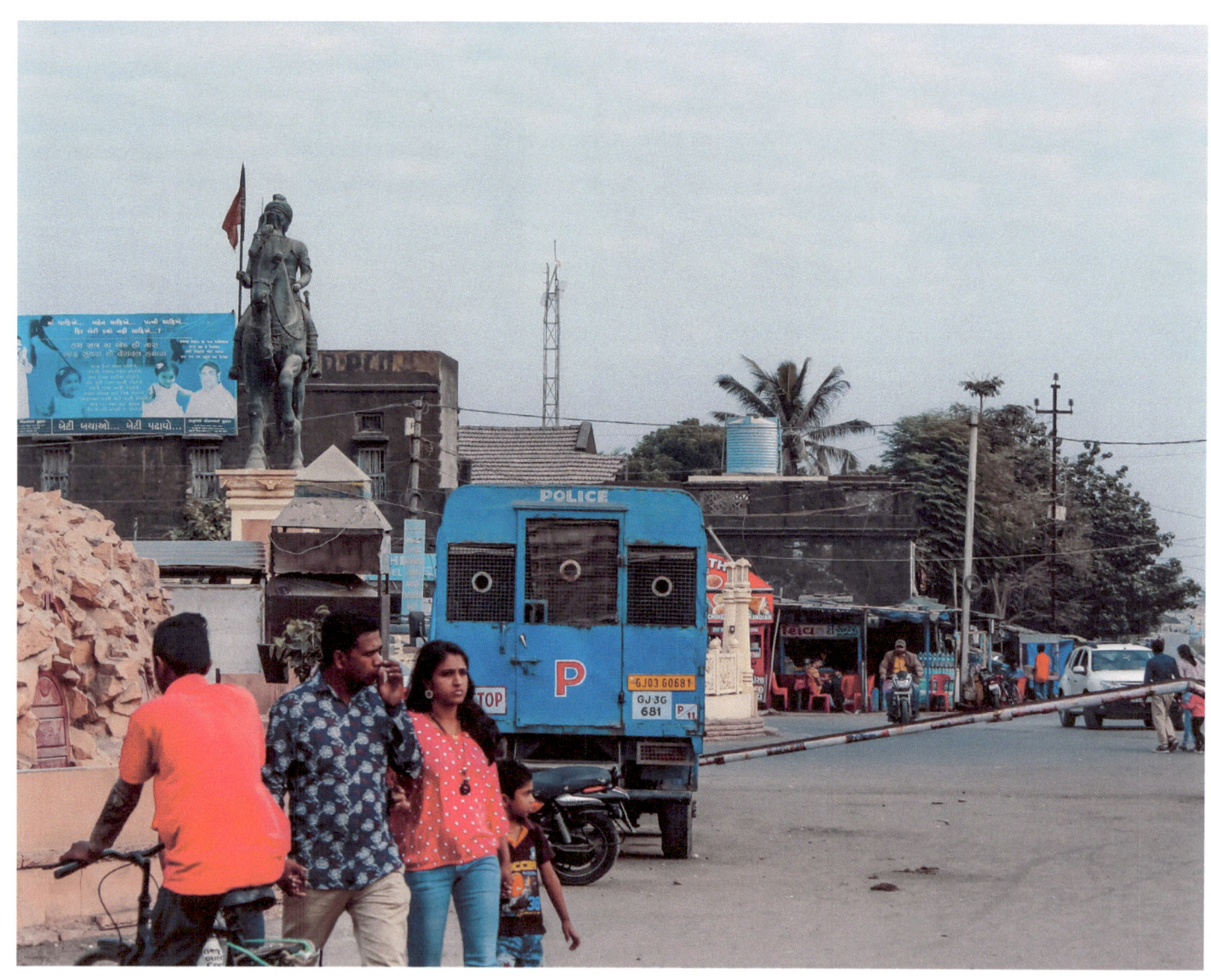

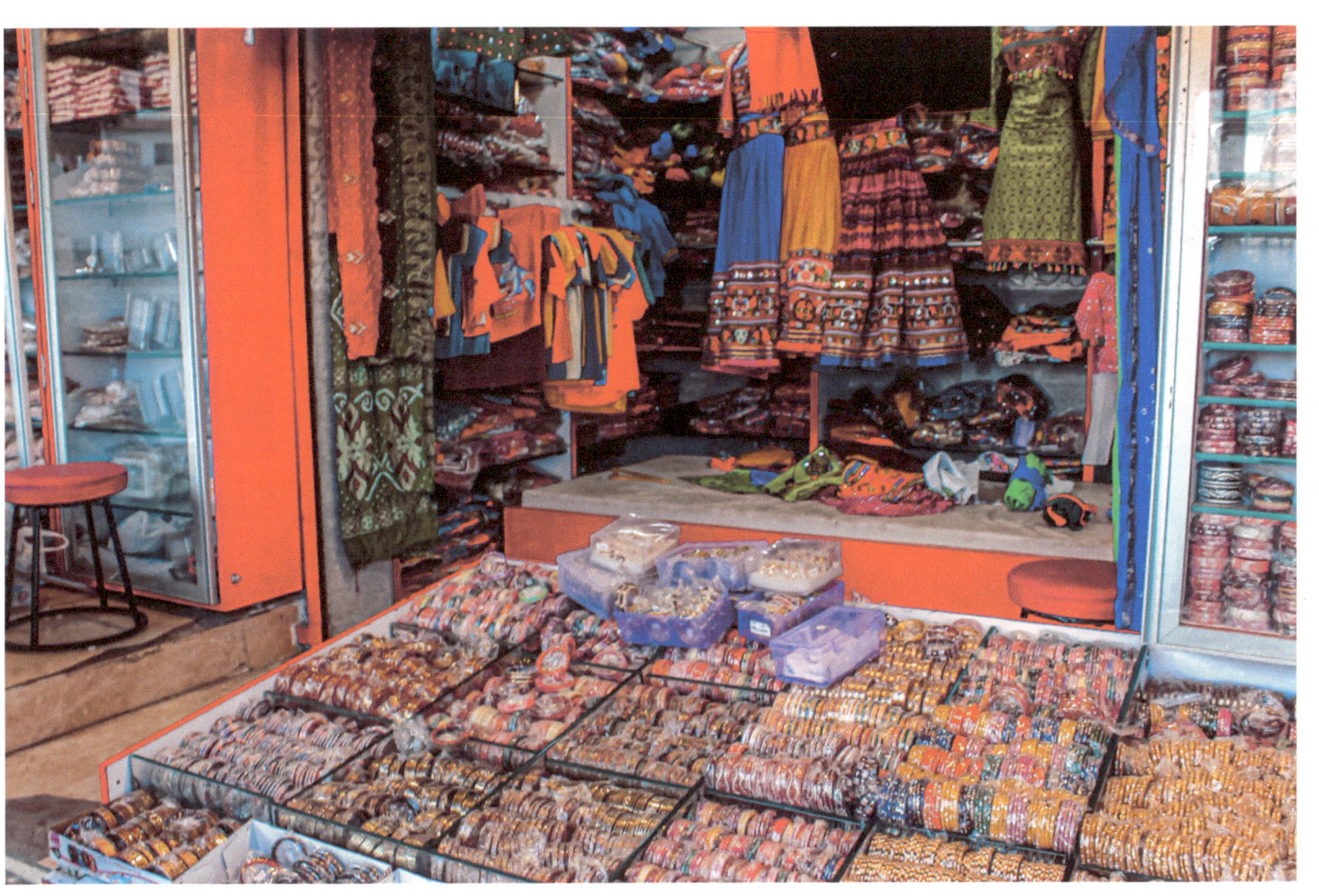

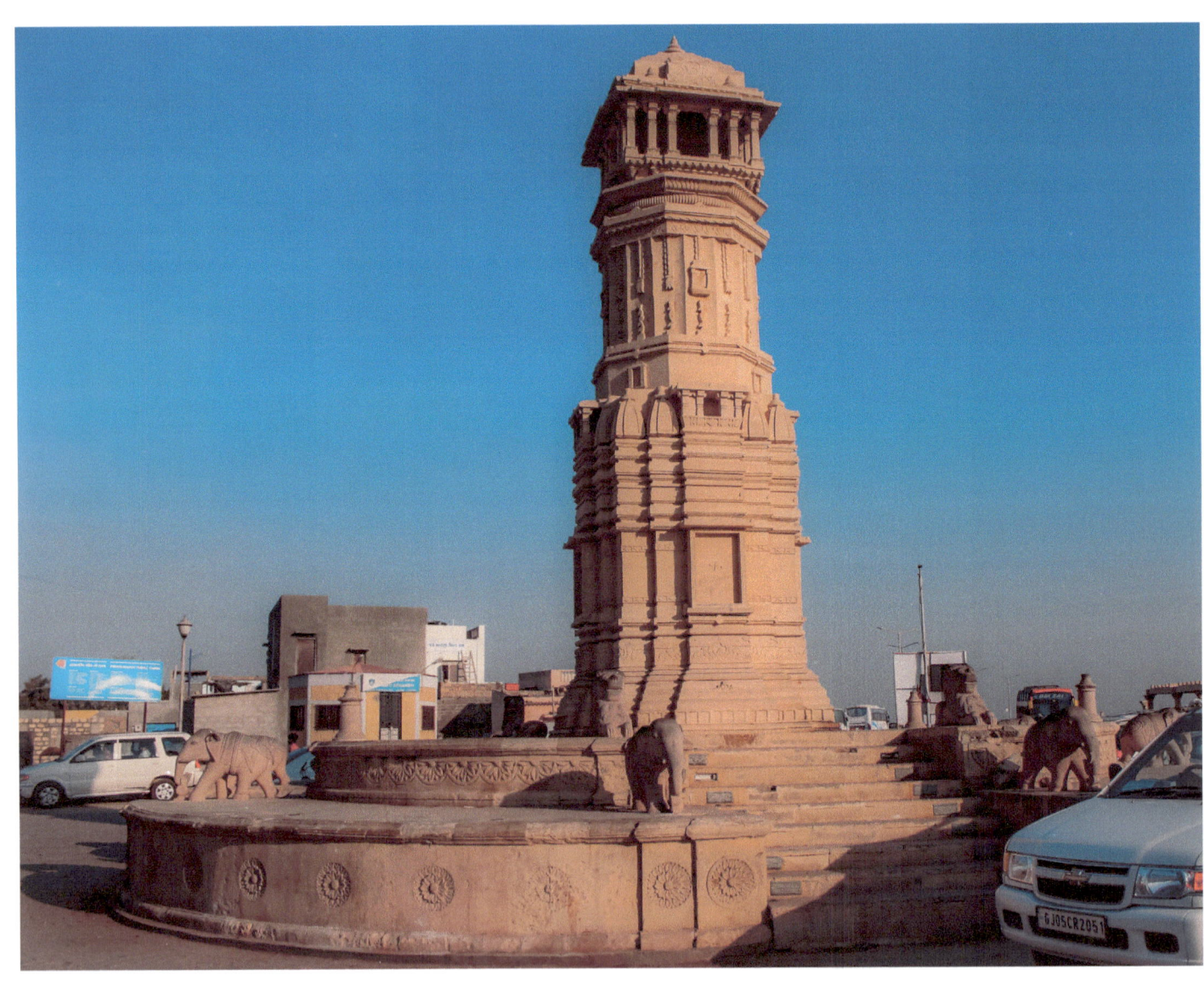

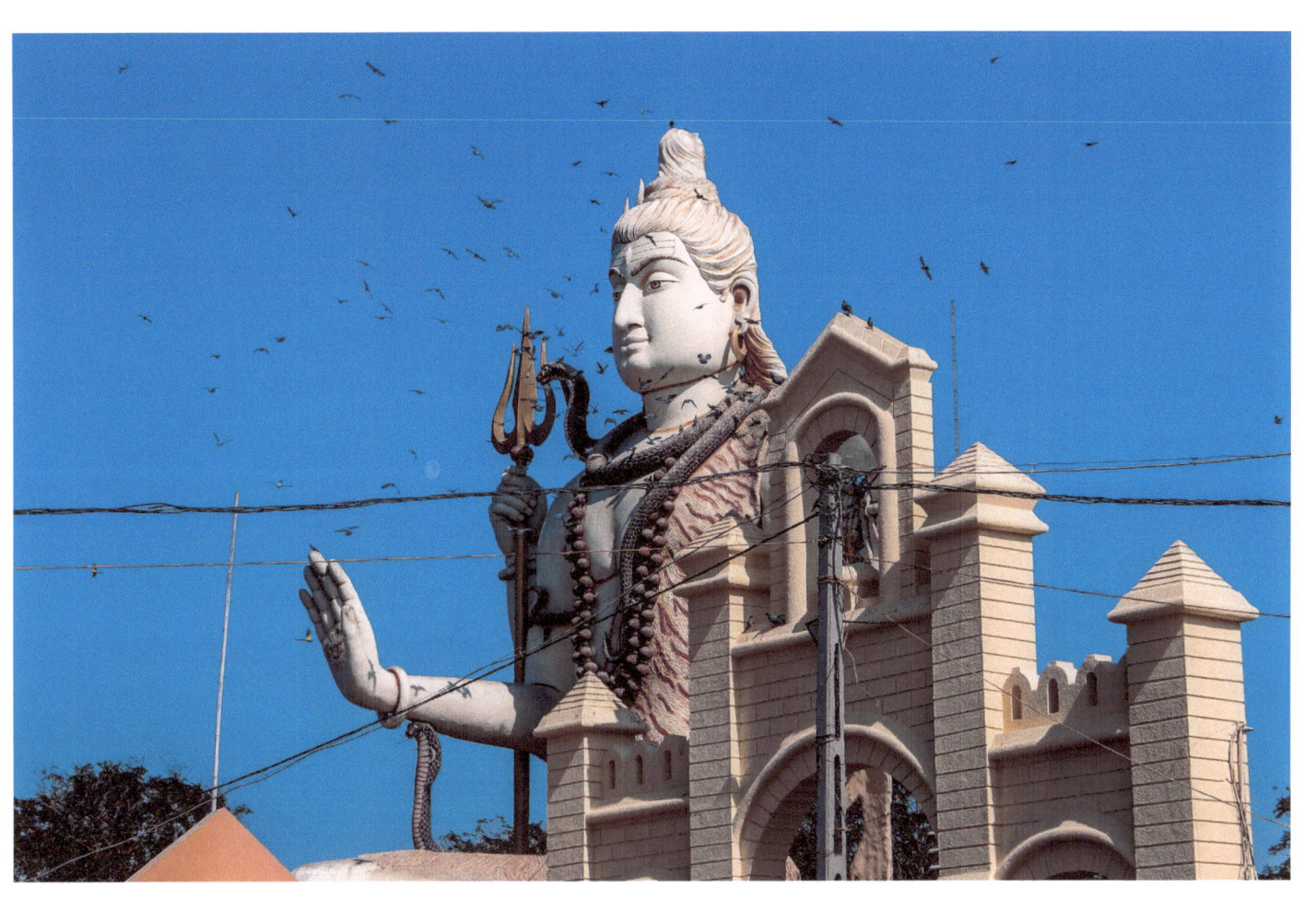

Porbandar, birth place of Sudama and Mahatma Gandhi...

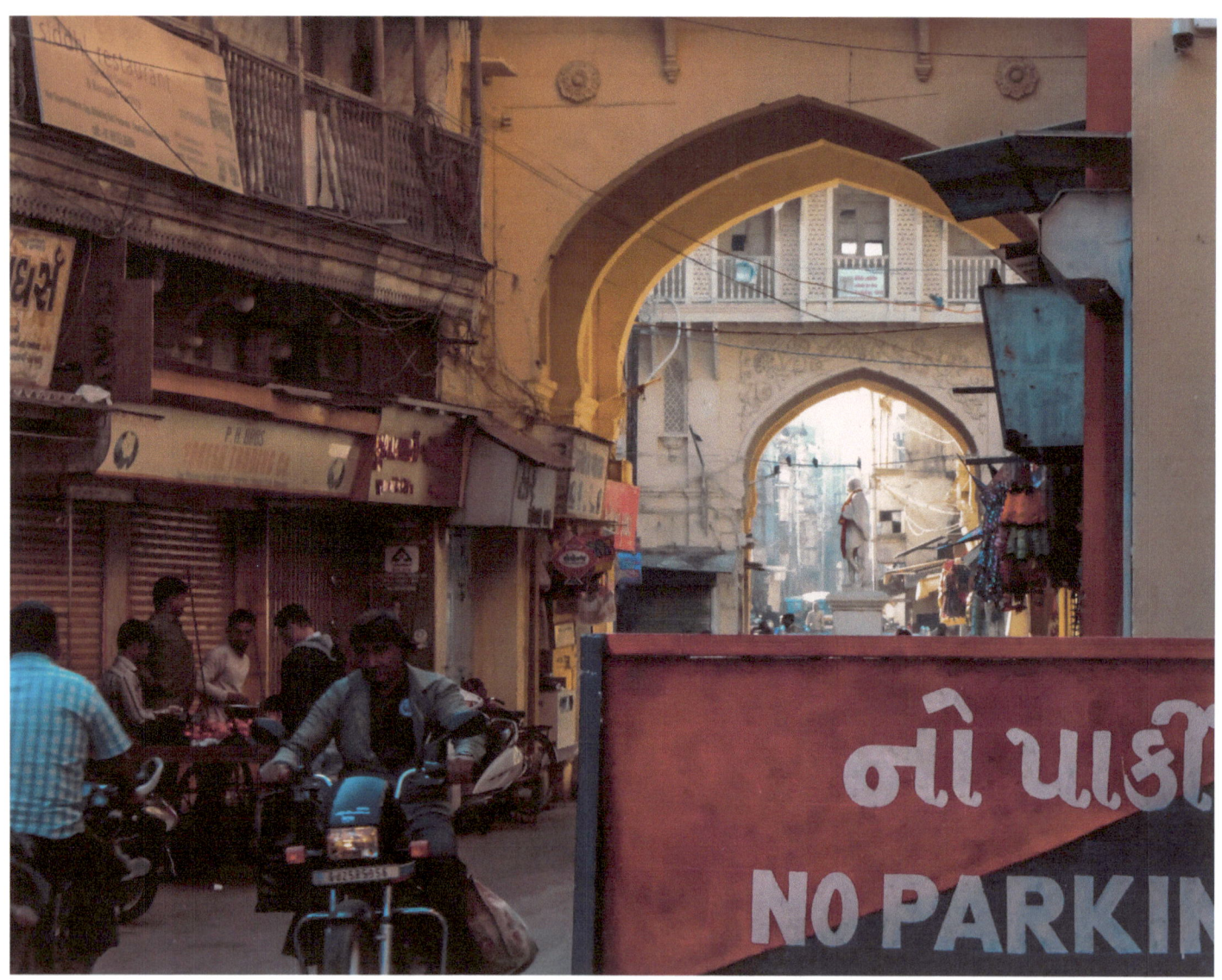

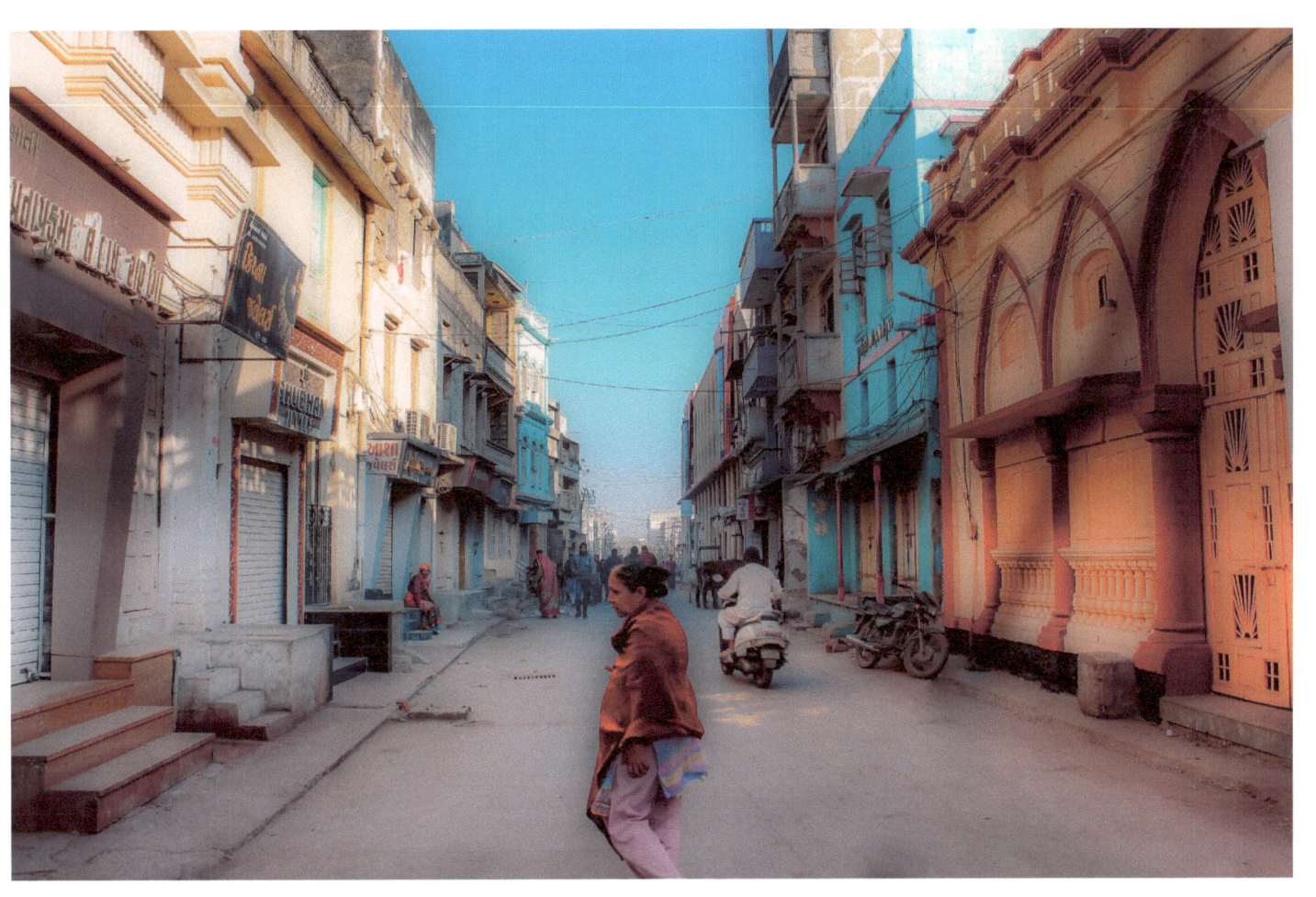

Mahatma Gandhi once peaked through these old windowns...

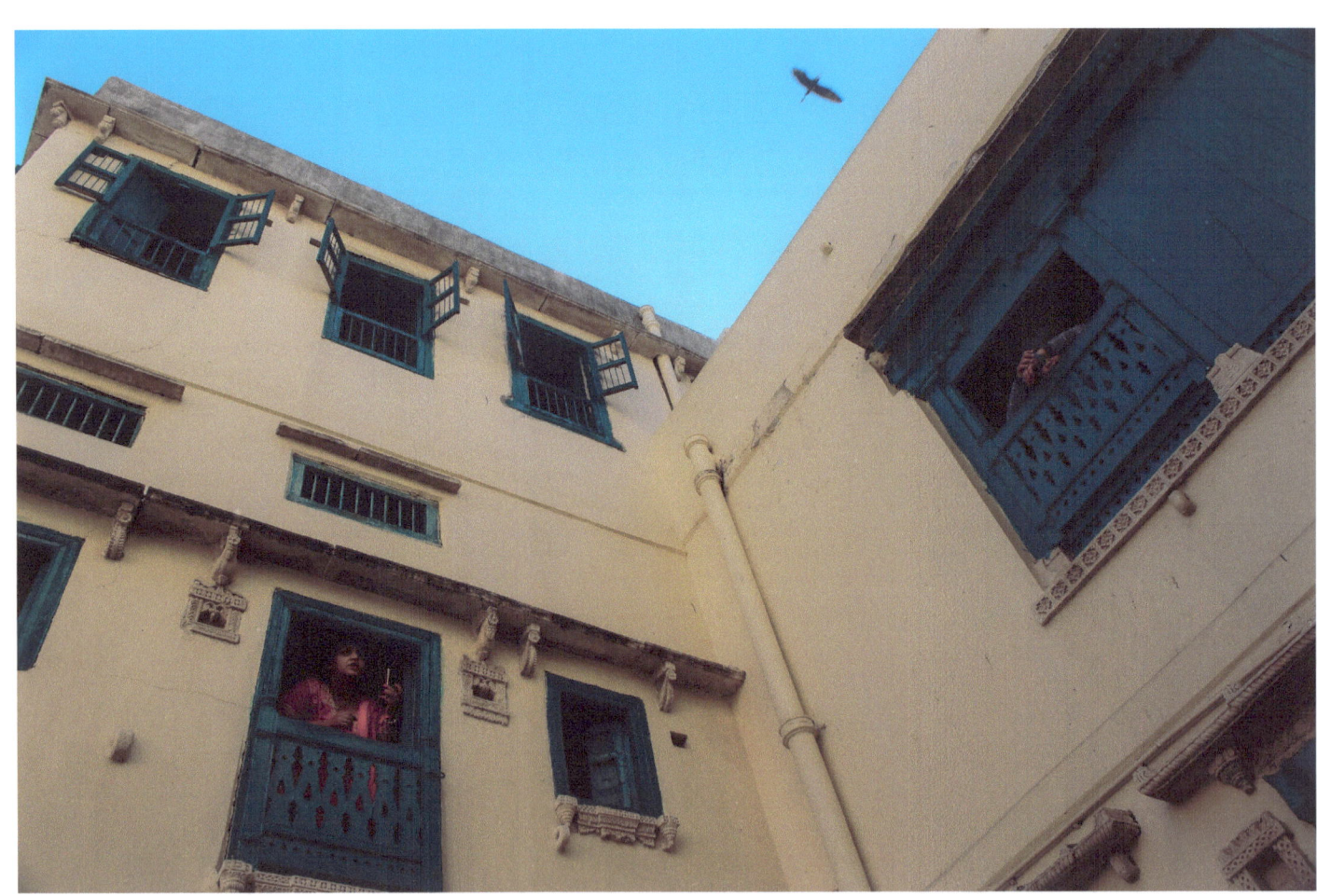

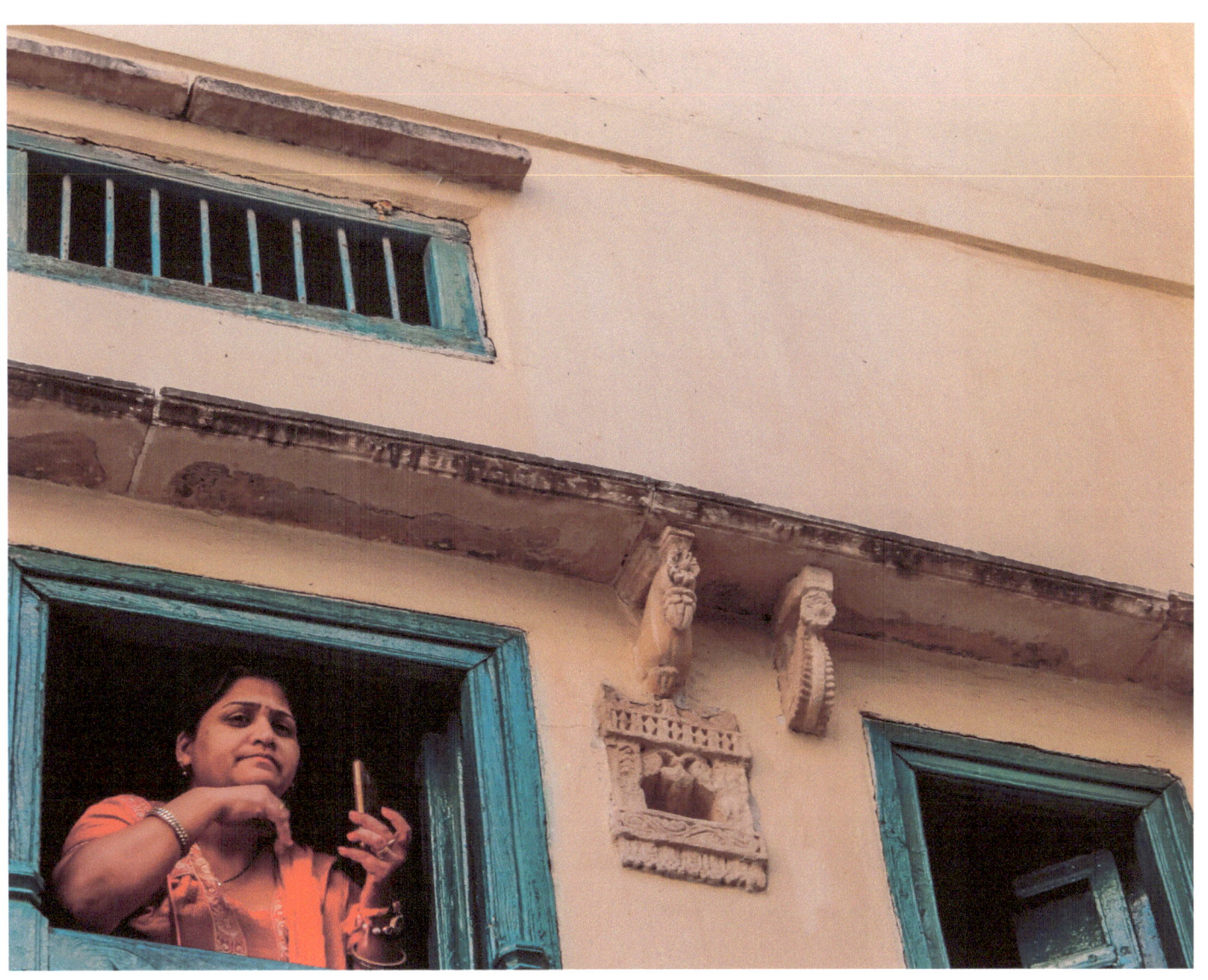

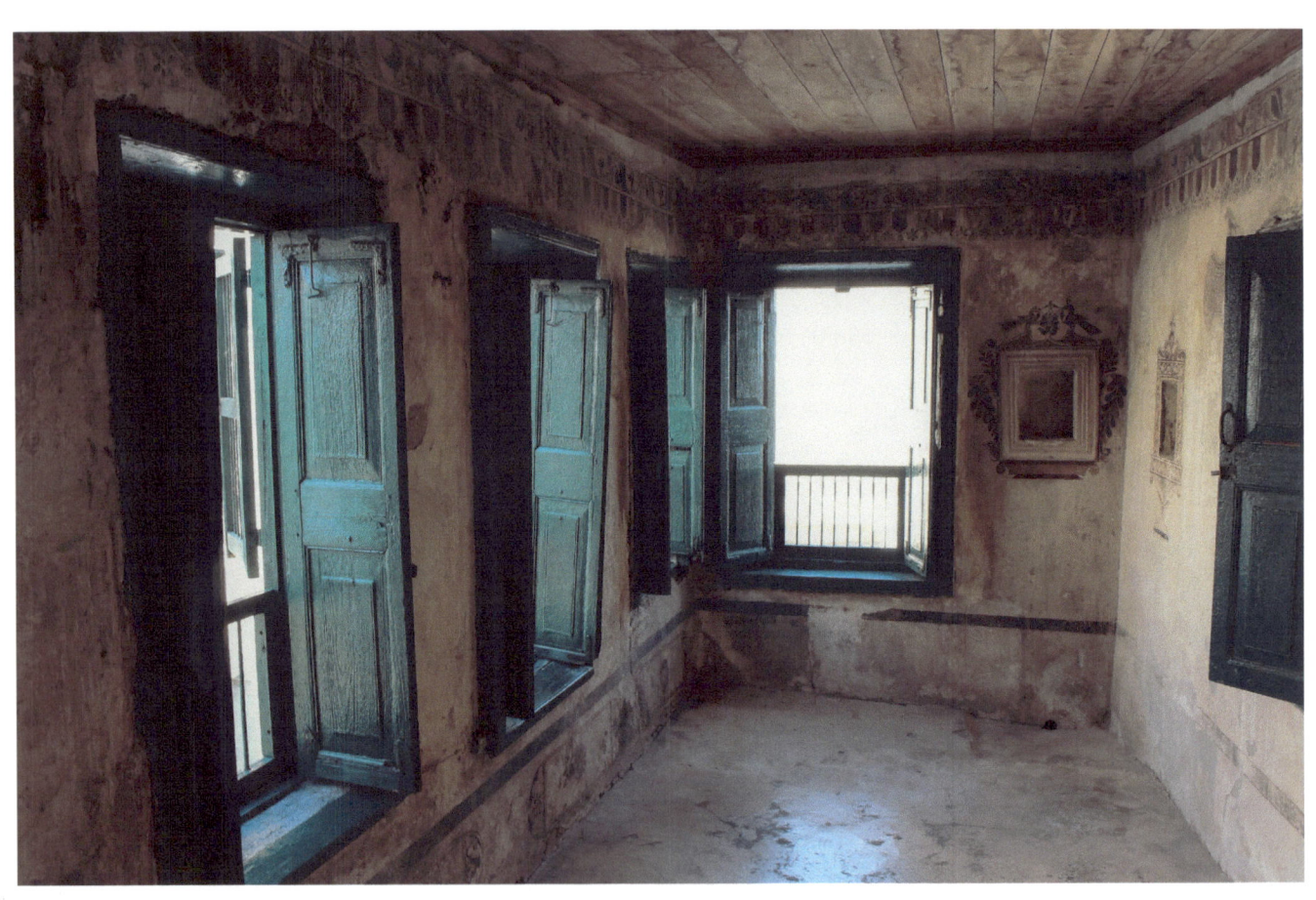

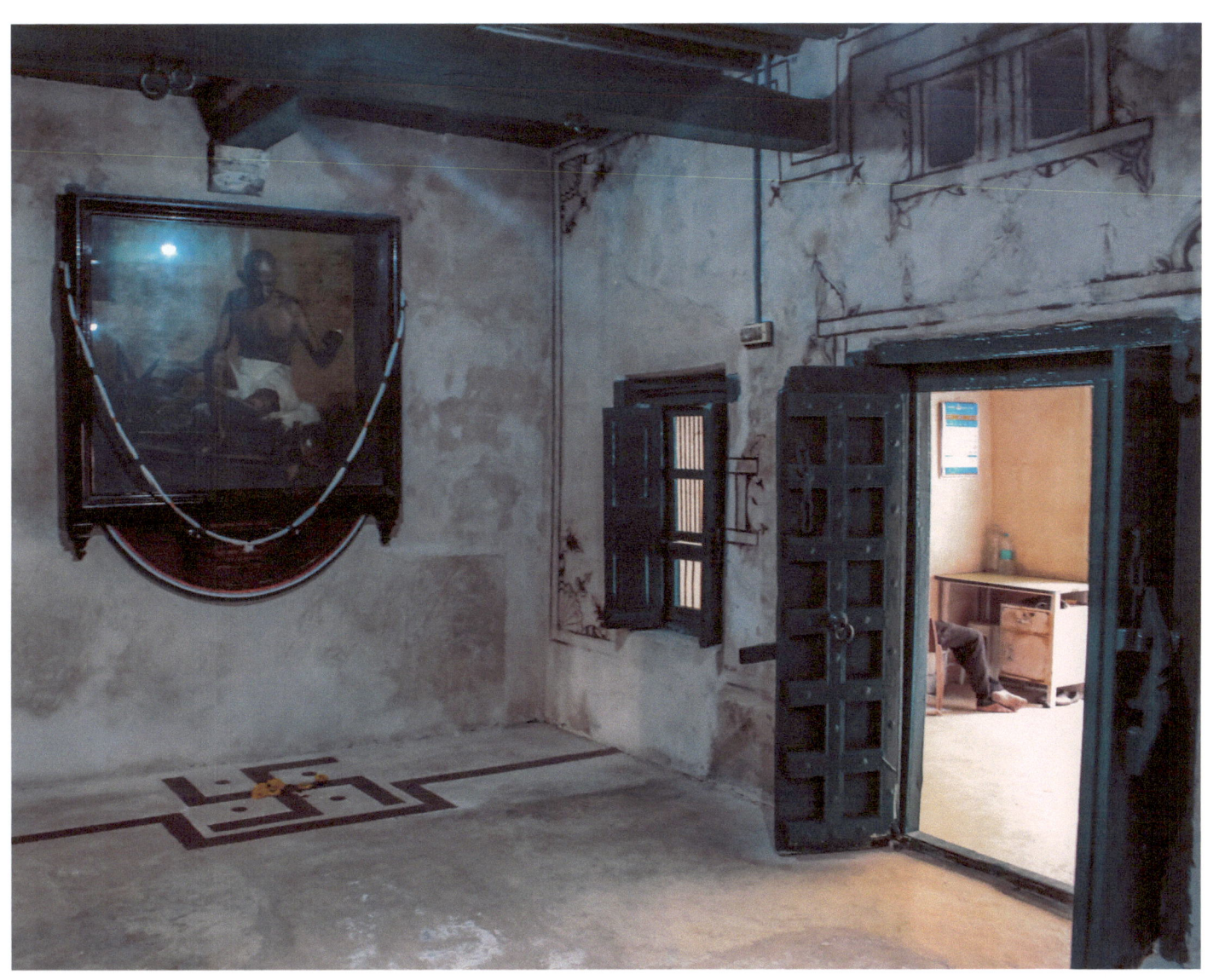

Krishna Sudama temple…

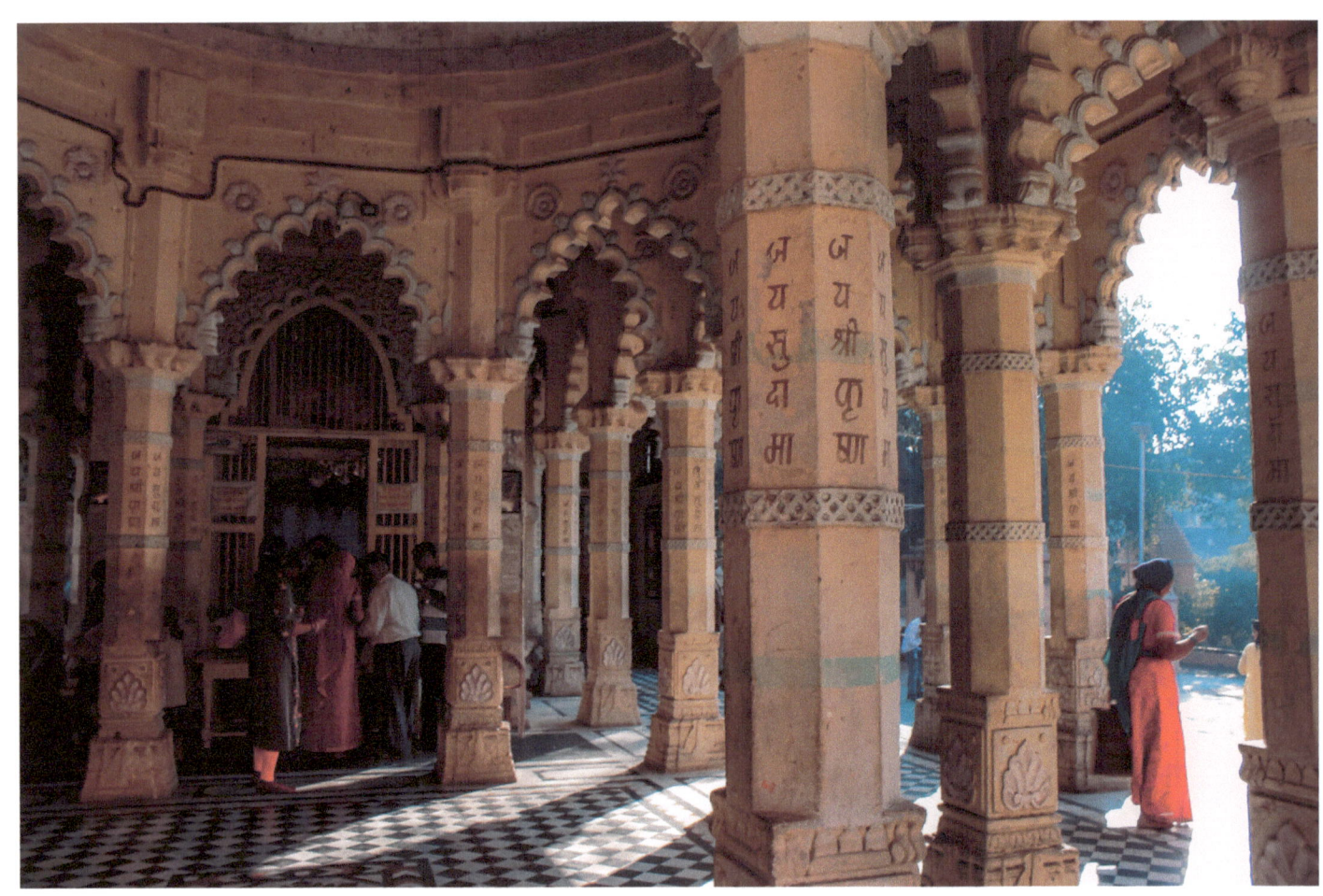

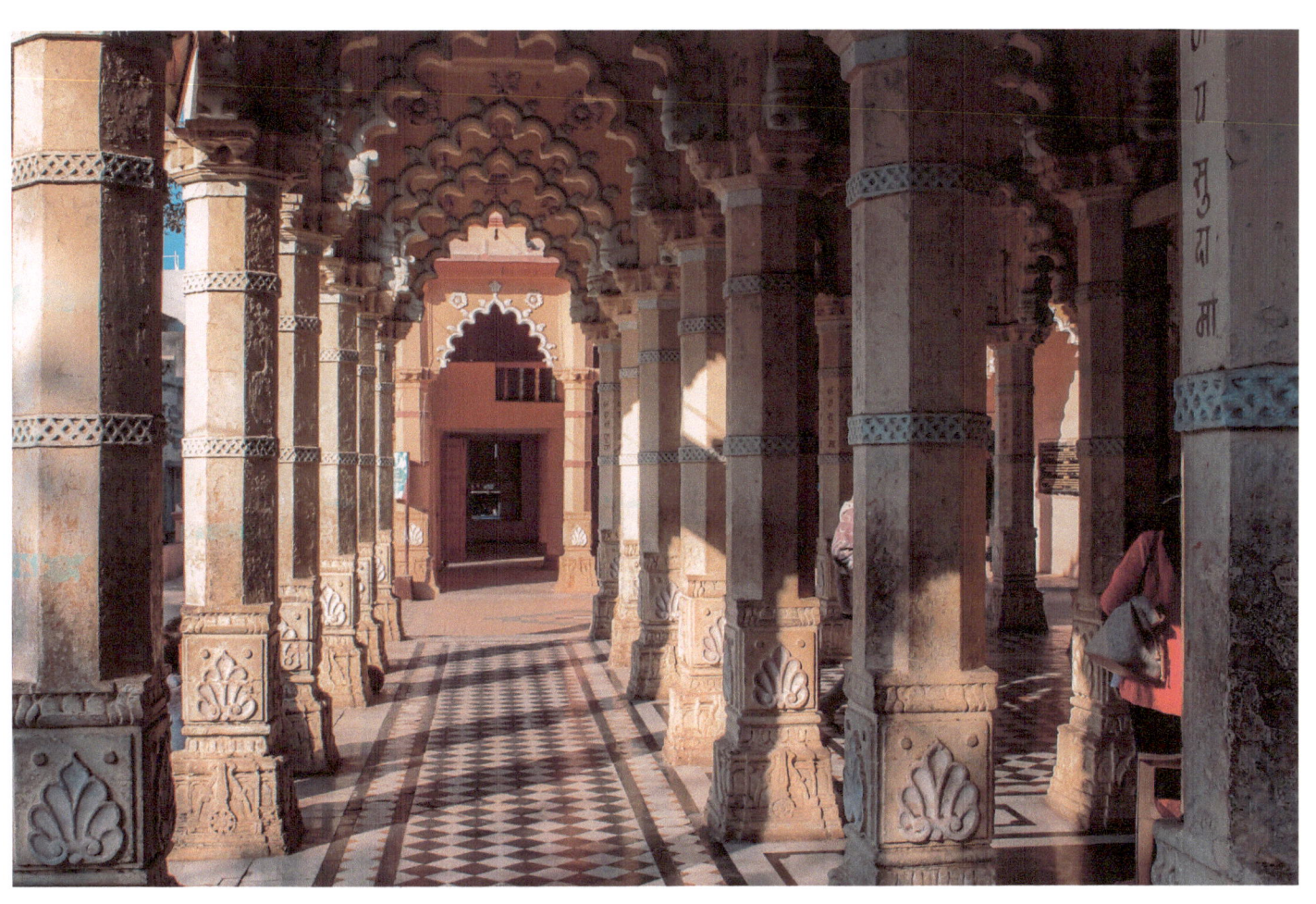

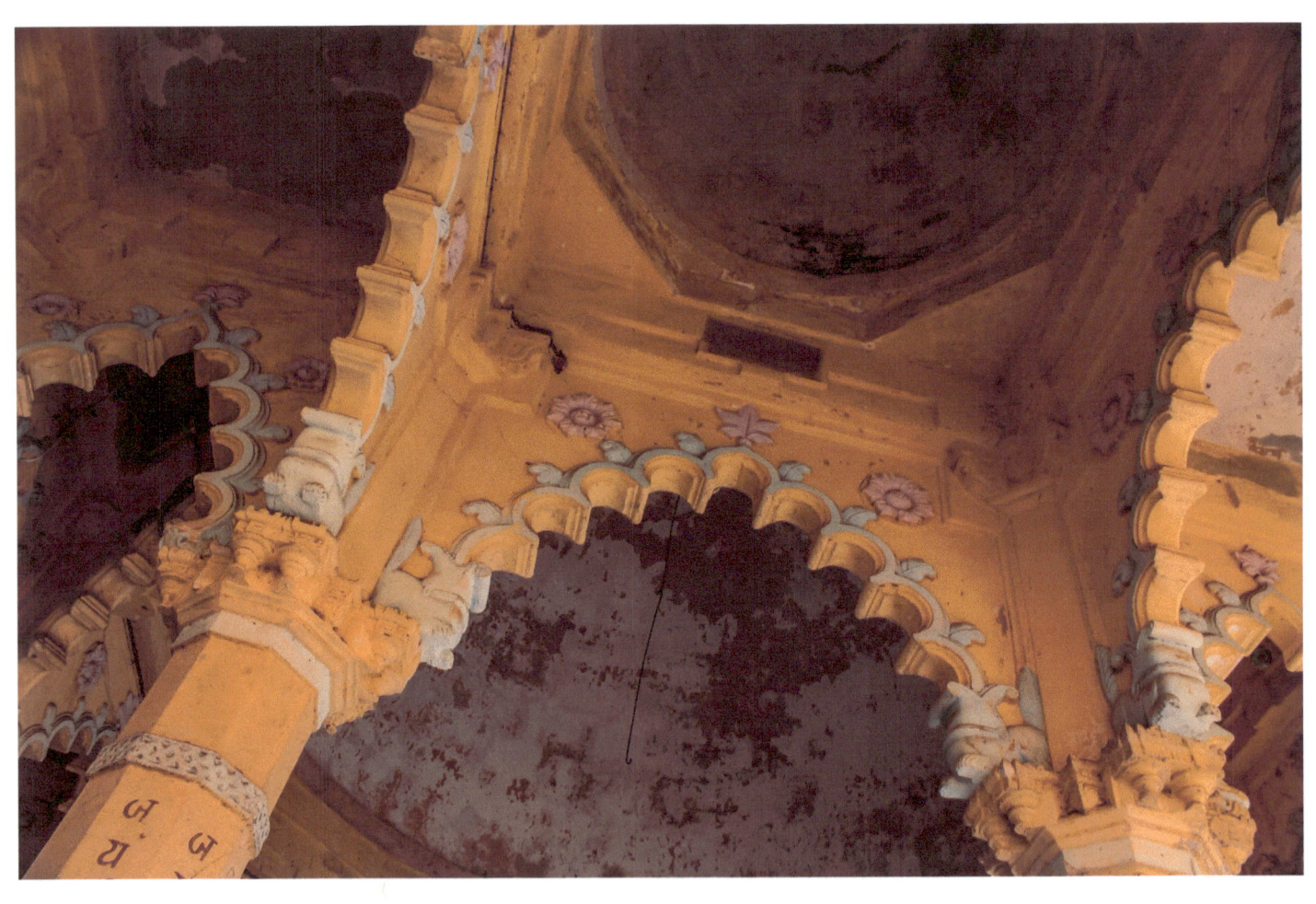

Locals praying and feeding the birds...

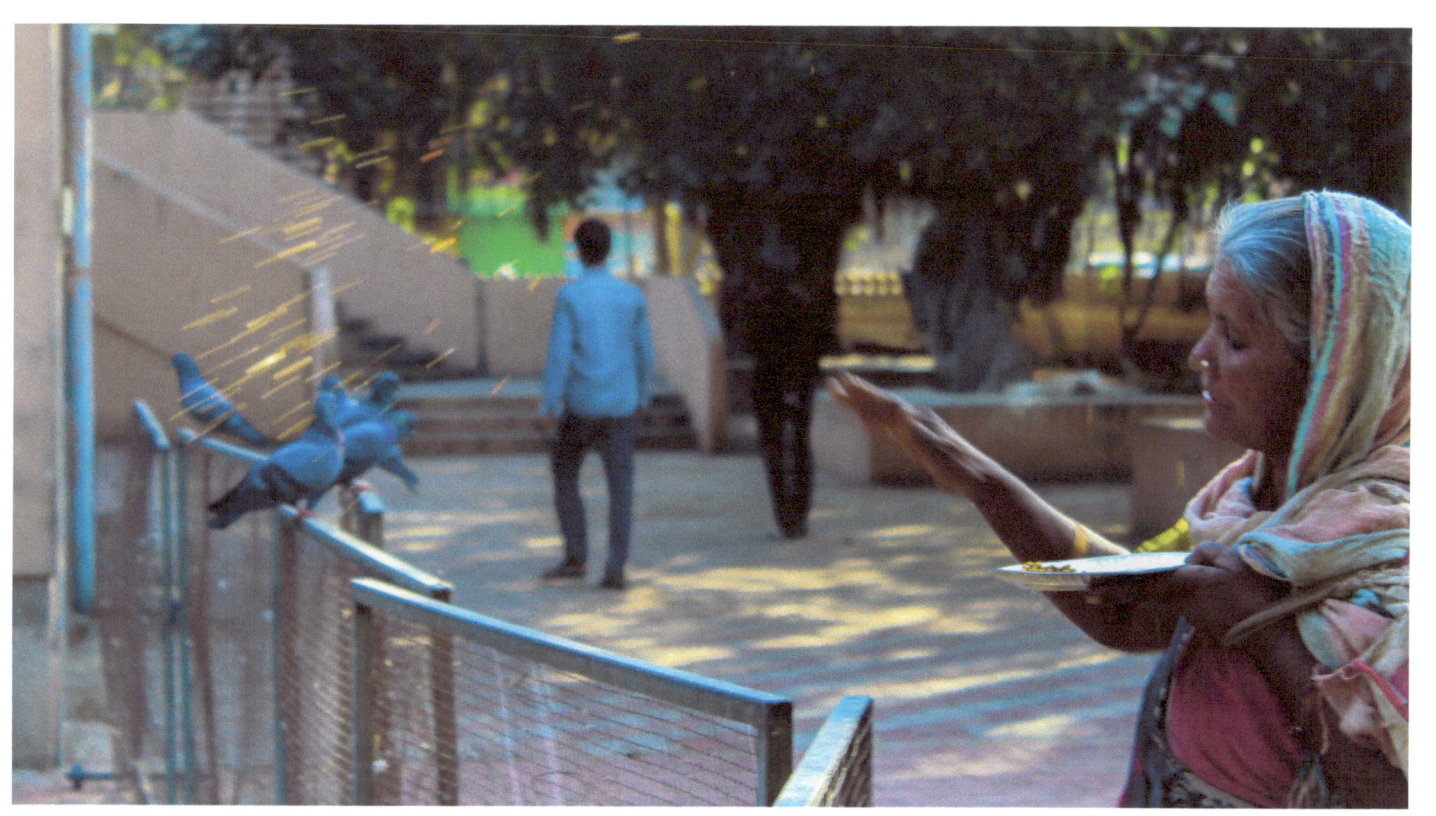

Preserved beaches of Madhavpur...

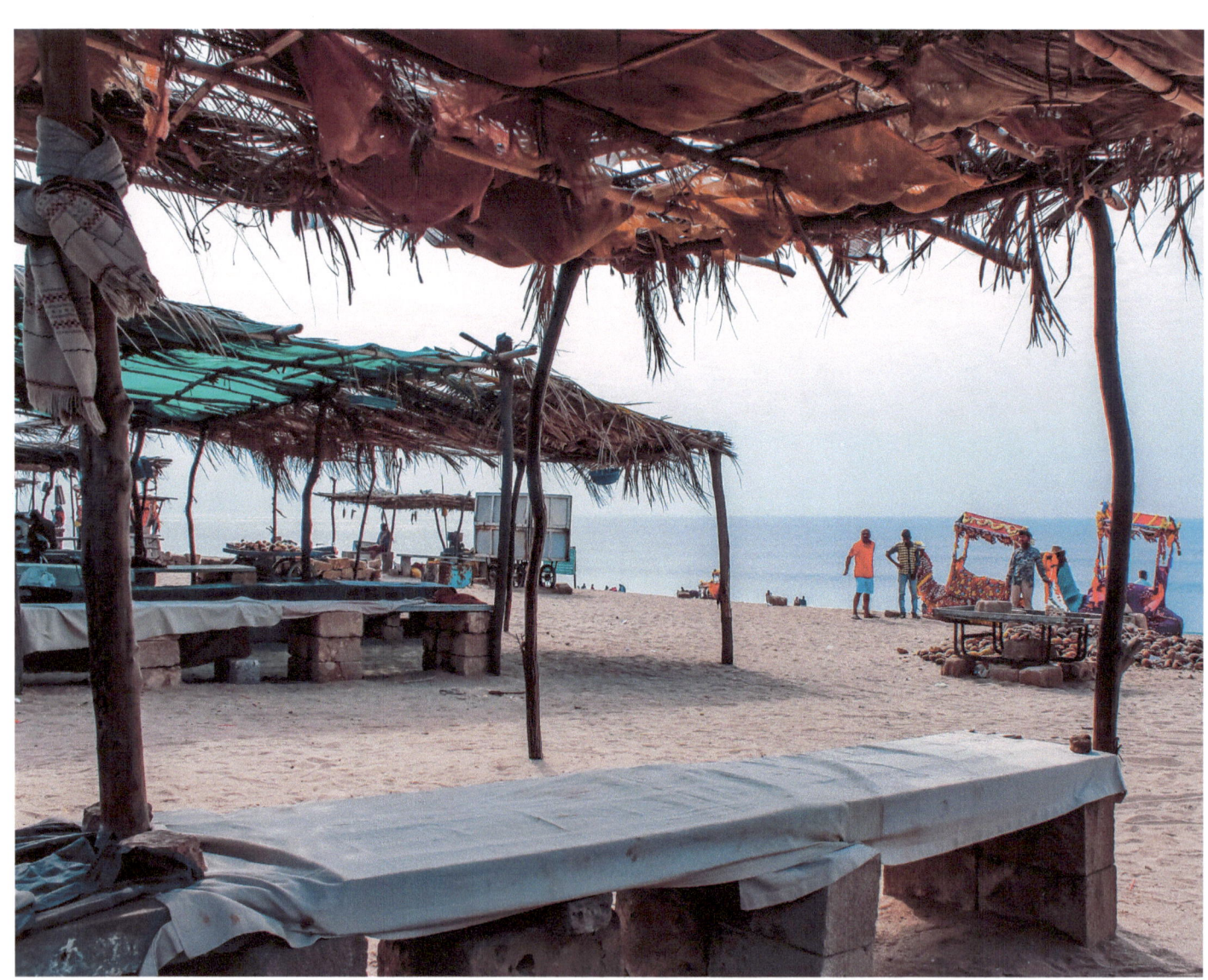

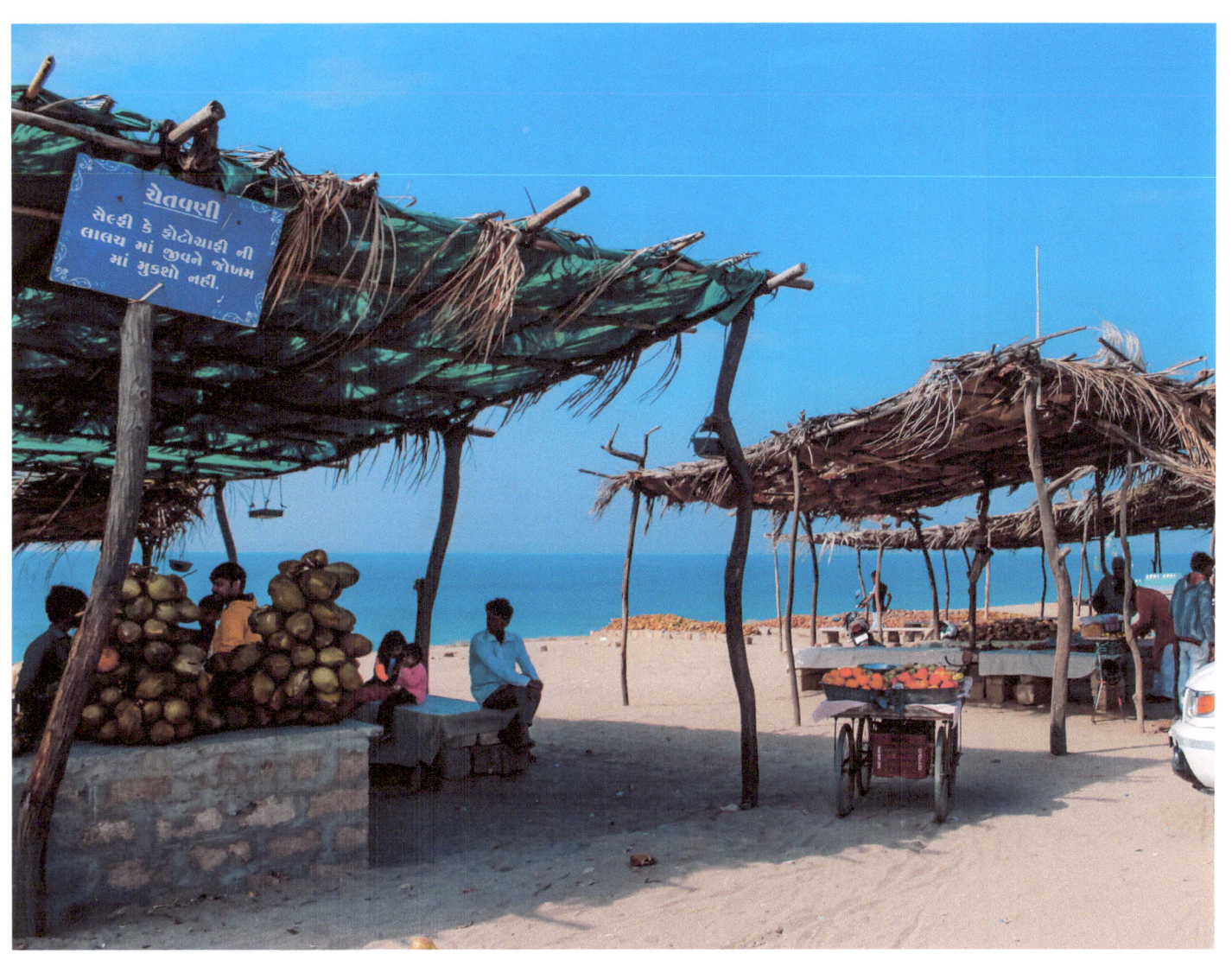

Street Vendors & Camel rides…

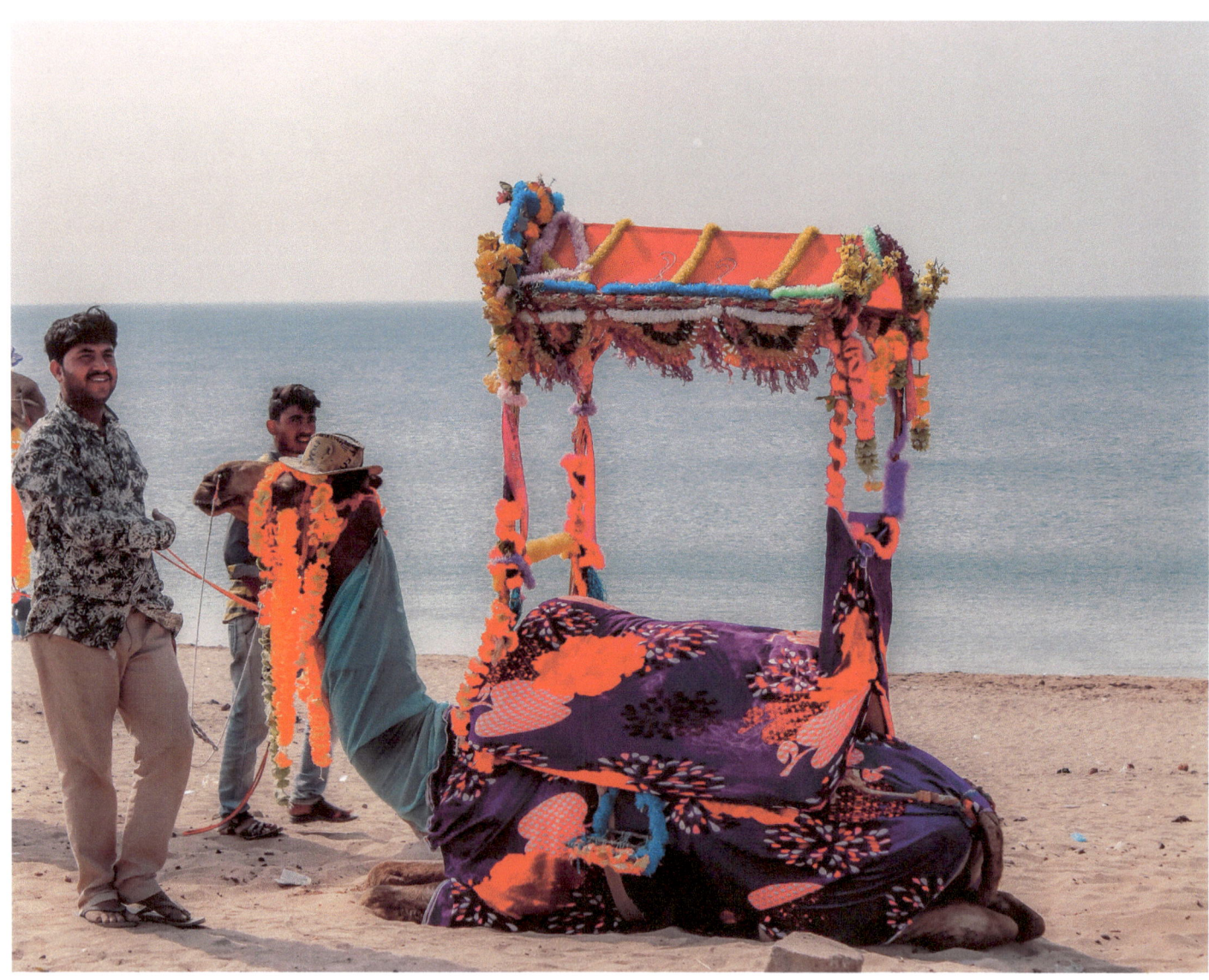

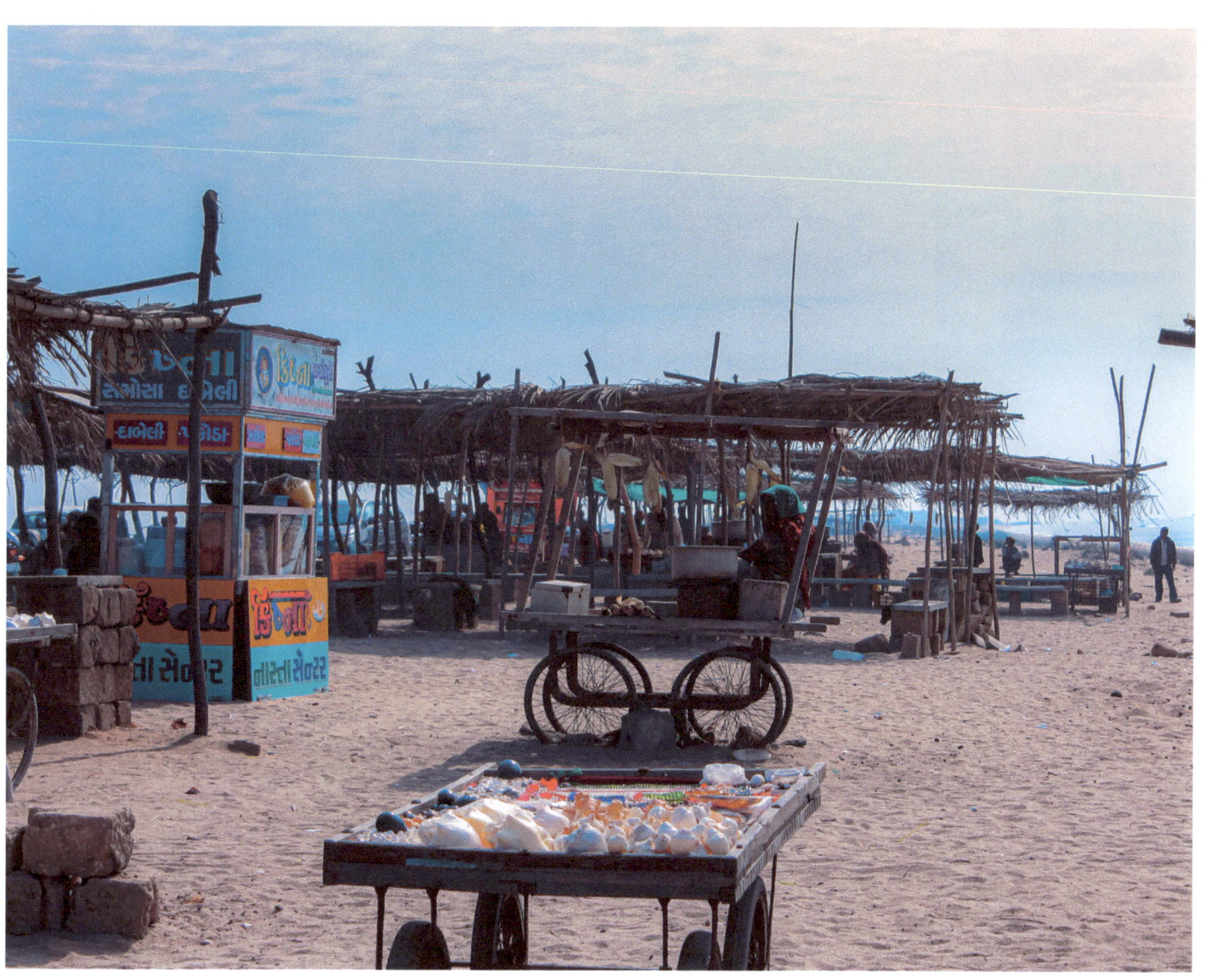

Somnath temple...

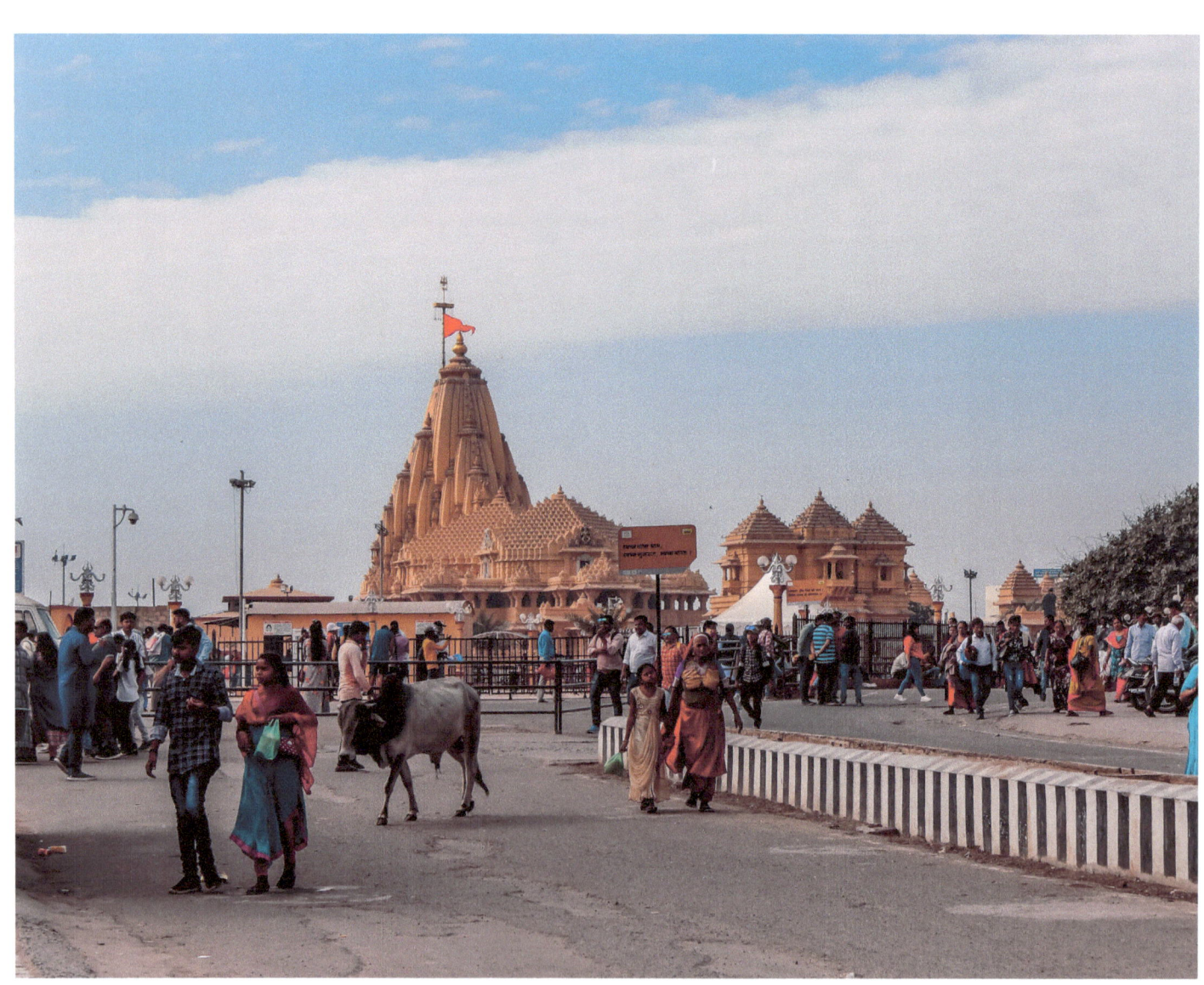

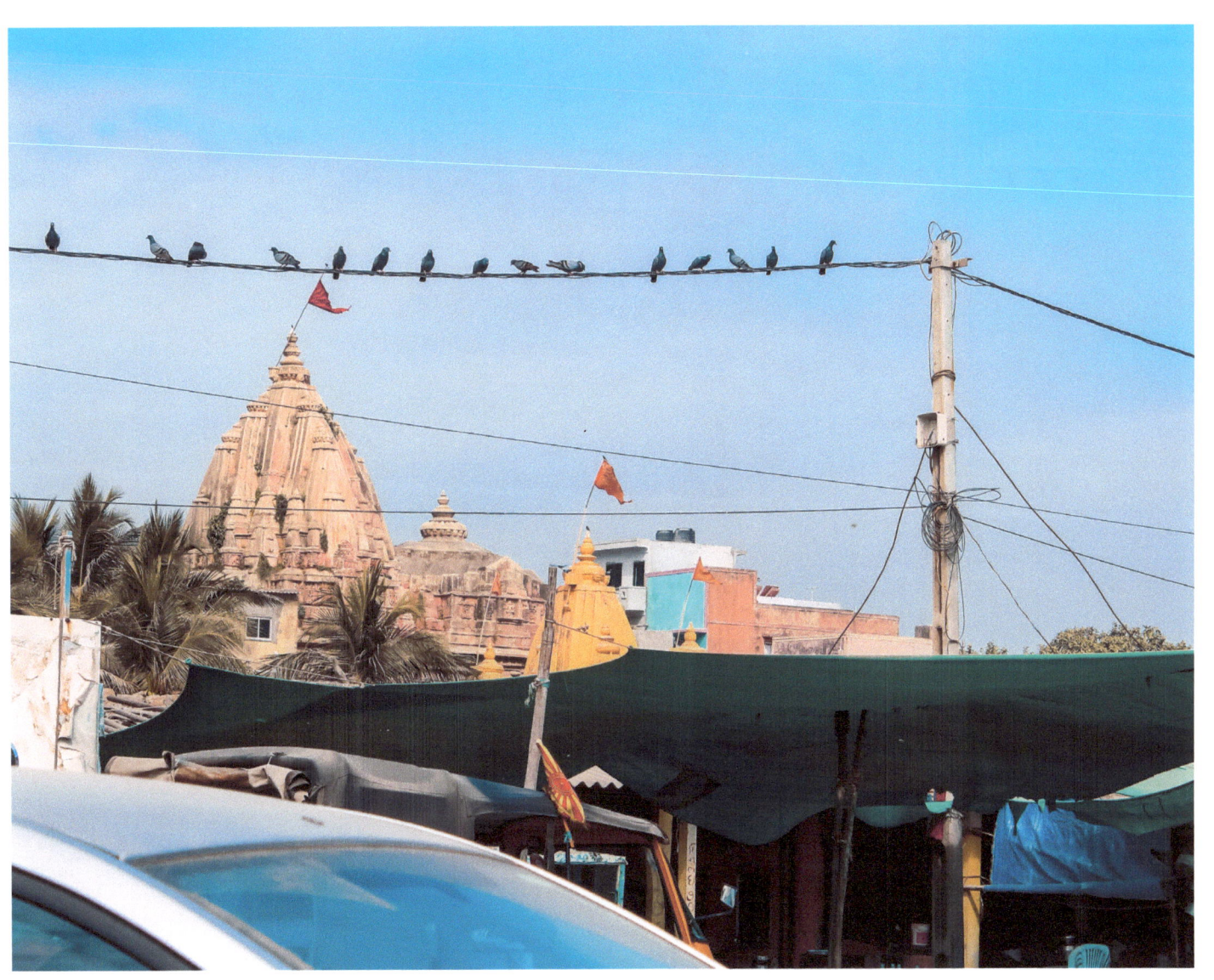

Serene temples and ponds...

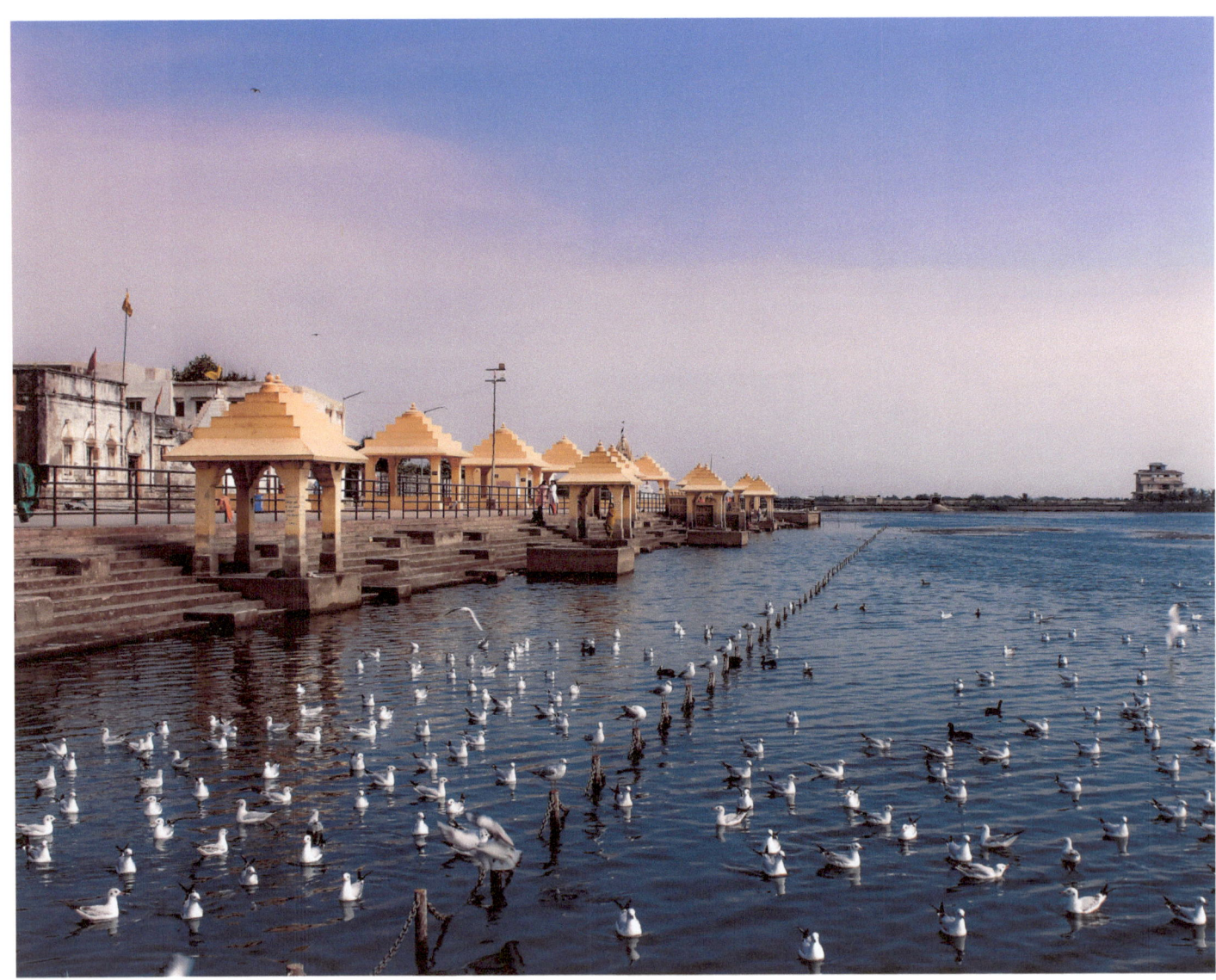

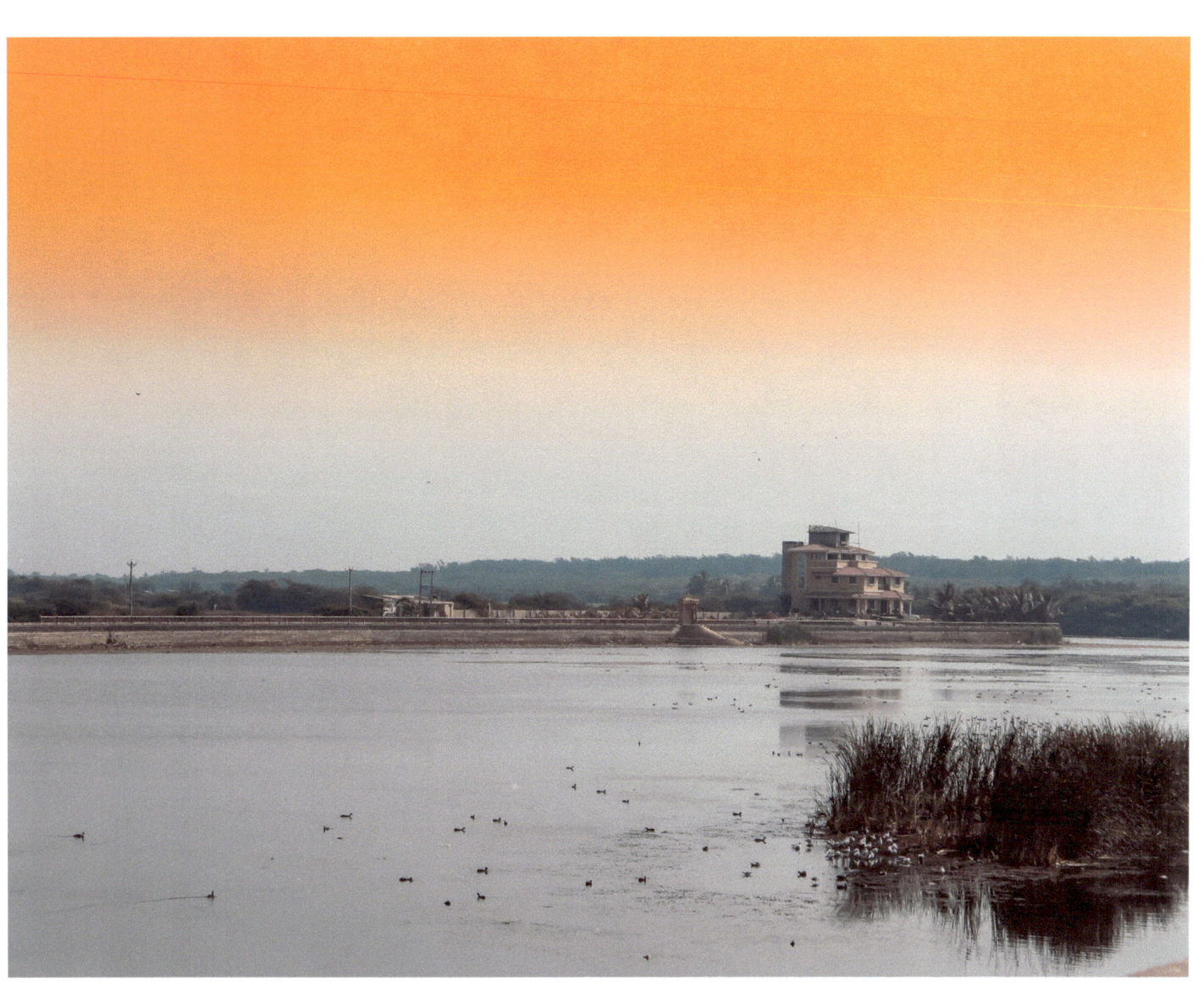

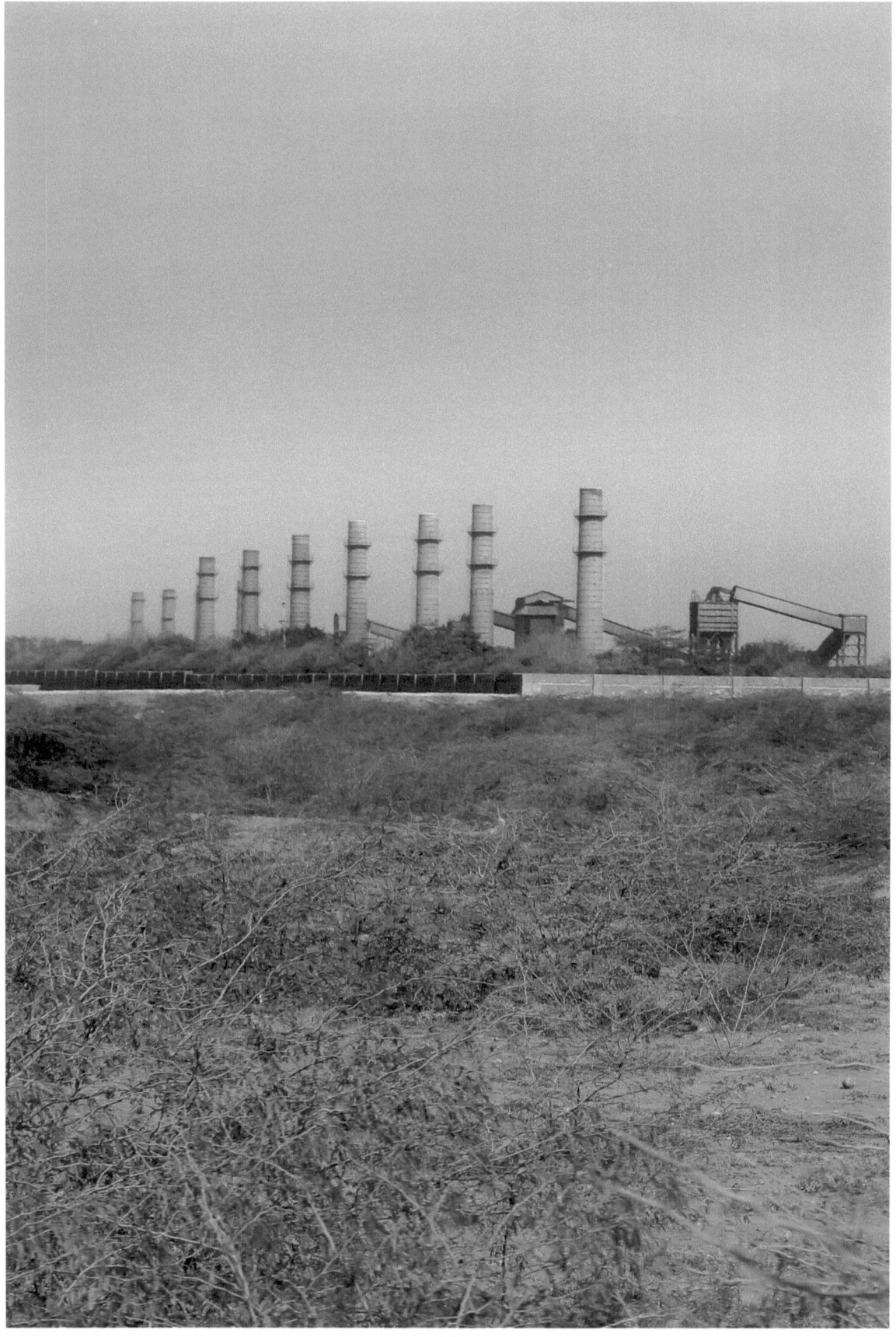

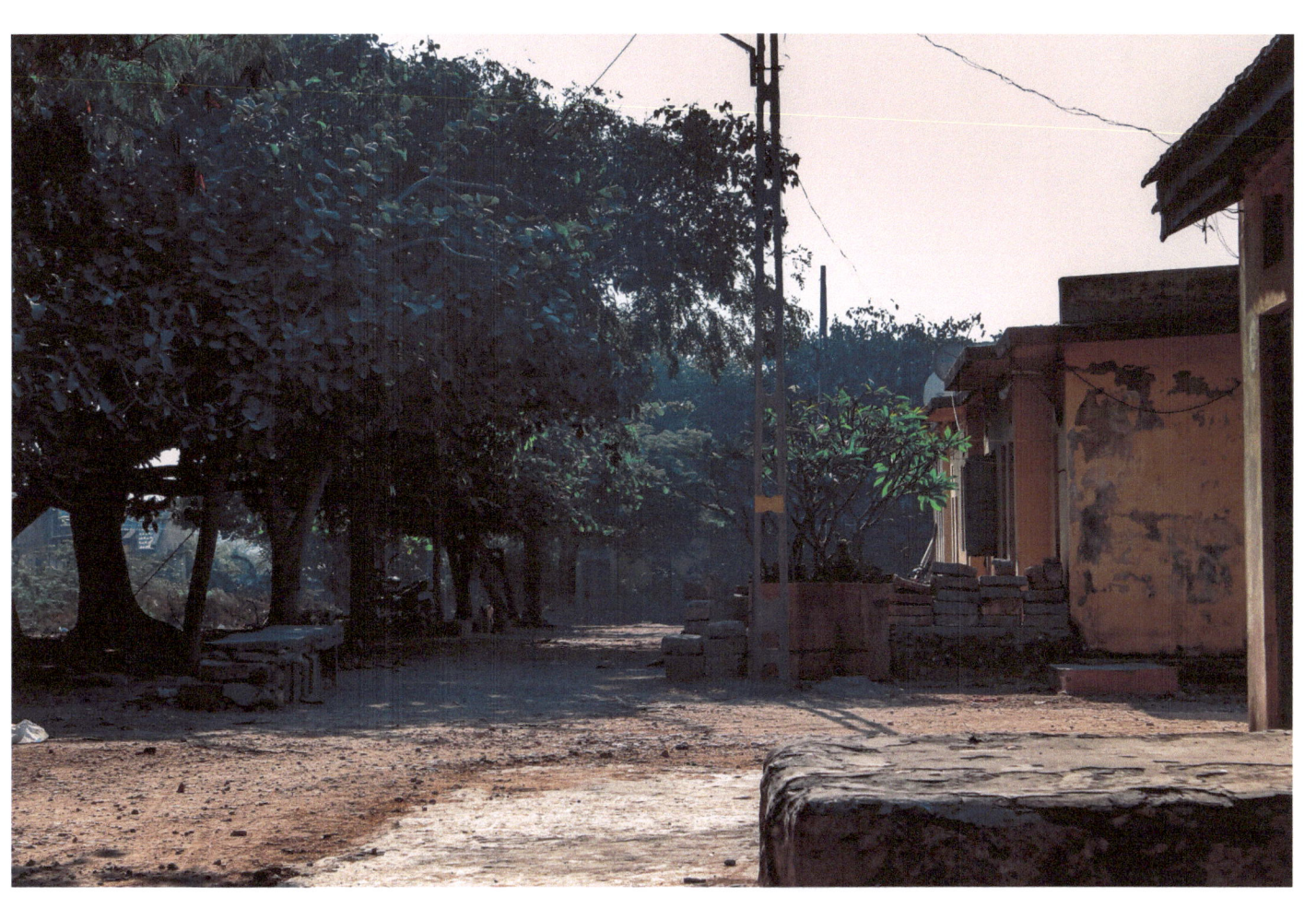

City of Gods, Phillaur, Punjab…

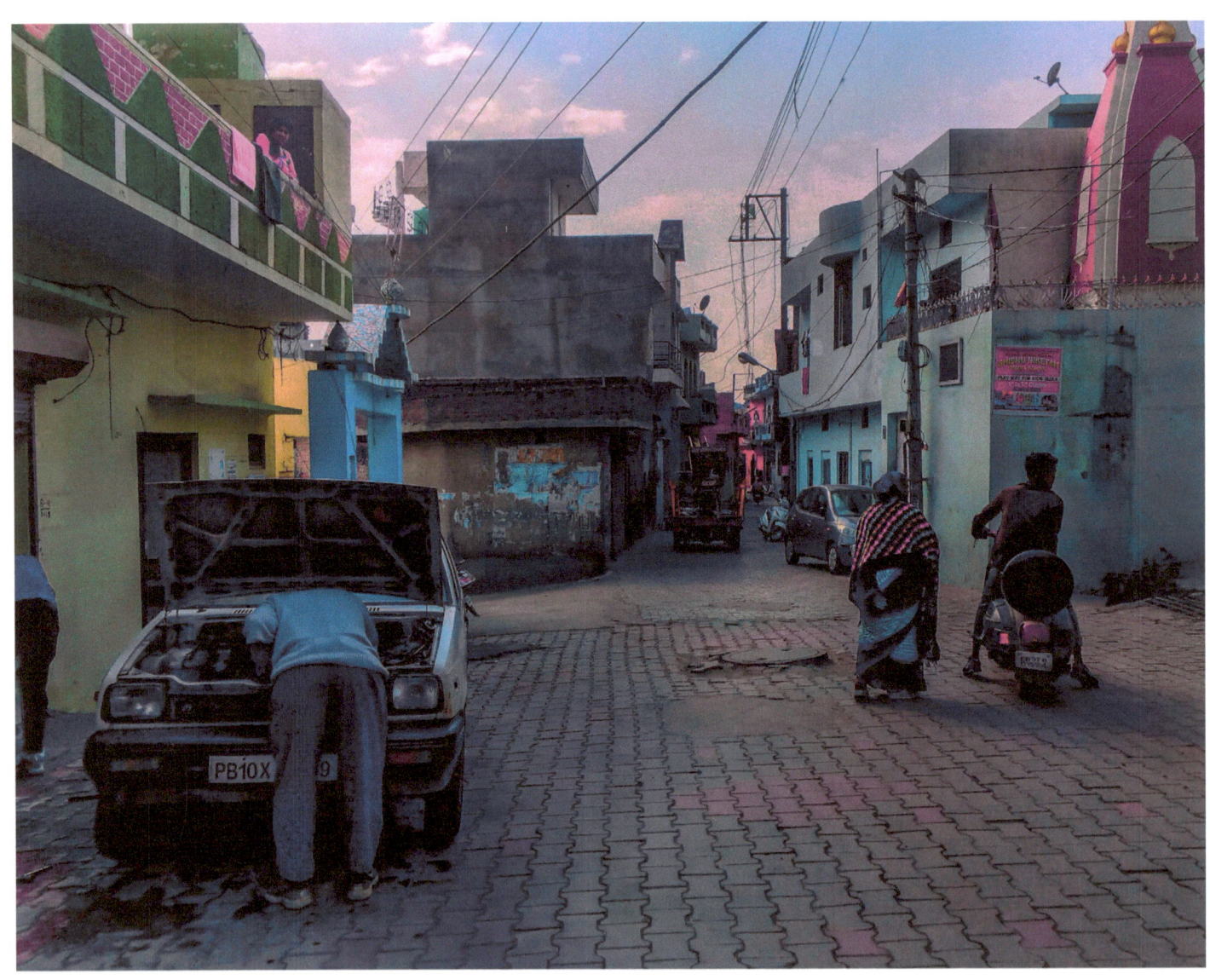

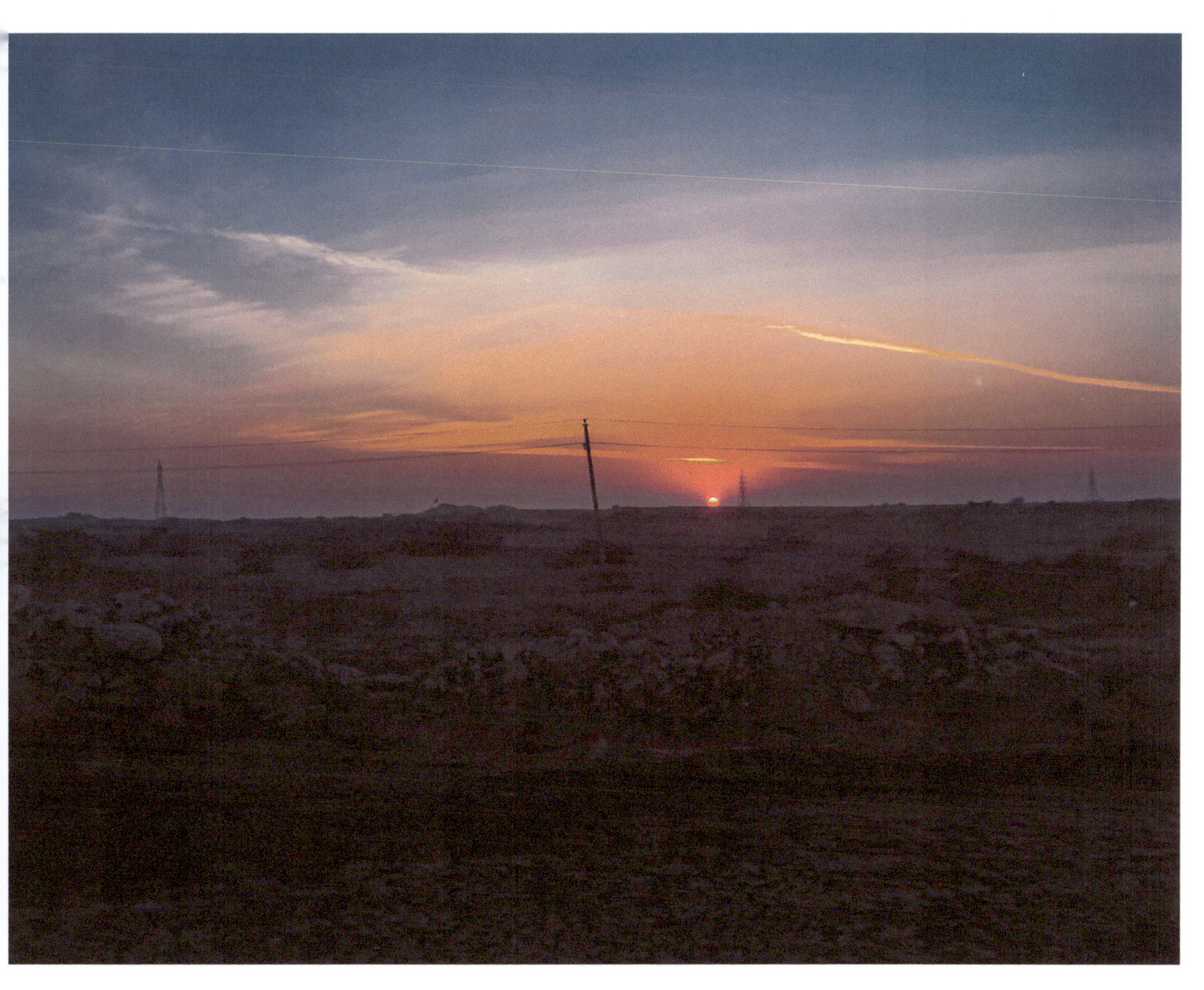

The end, a new journey begins…

www.ingramcontent.com/pod-product-compliance
Lightning Source LLC
Chambersburg PA
CBHW051209220526
45473CB00003B/969